To Mike,
The best is ˃

God's Grace and Biblical Faith

A Revelation of God's Love

Stephen J. Pitts 2/26/23

Stephen J. Pitts

TRILOGY

God's Grace and Biblical Faith: A Revelation of God's Love
Trilogy Christian Publishers A Wholly Owned Subsidiary of Trinity
Broadcasting Network
2442 Michelle Drive Tustin, CA 92780
Rights Department, 2442 Michelle Drive, Tustin, CA 92780.
Trilogy Christian Publishing/TBN and colophon are trademarks of Trinity
Broadcasting Network.
Cover design by: ~~Josh Crow~~ Stephen Pitts w/Josh Crow
For information about special discounts for bulk purchases, please contact
Trilogy Christian Publishing.
Trilogy Disclaimer: The views and content expressed in this book are
those of the author and may not necessarily reflect the views and doctrine
of Trilogy Christian Publishing or the Trinity Broadcasting Network.
Manufactured in the United States of America

10 9 8 7 6 5 4 3 2 1

Library of Congress Cataloging-in-Publication Data is available.
ISBN: 978-1-68556-829-0
E-ISBN: 978-1-68556-830-6

**This book is dedicated to
the glory of God: our Heavenly Father
and His living Word/Jesus Christ.**

Table of Contents

Introduction

As the years go by, the sobering reality of the following scripture becomes more and more apparent: "Whereas ye know not what *shall be* on the morrow. For what *is* your life? It is even a vapour, that appeareth for a little time, and then vanisheth away" (James 4:14). With that in mind, it helps us realize how important it is to have a personal, spiritual relationship with Jesus Christ. We need to understand that this is a love relationship with God that comes by knowing Jesus Christ as our Lord and Savior, and knowing Him comes by receiving His spiritual truth. How can we believe in Jesus Christ and rely on Him for salvation if we don't know and love Him? The diligent and heartfelt Bible study that went along with writing this book is how I came to know and love our Lord and Savior Jesus Christ. "Jesus answered and said unto him, If a man love me, he will keep my words: and my Father will love him, and we will come unto him, and make our abode with him" (John 14:23).

When I look back on my life, I can clearly see that God's love has always been there for me even though I didn't deserve it: I ignored the truth and moral standard of God's living Word/ Jesus Christ for many years, but His amazing grace continued to call to me and bless me every step of the way.

My earliest memories associated with Christianity date back to when I was seven years old. One of the neighbor ladies started having Bible studies for children at her house, and even though I don't remember much about them, I do have a vague memory of being there, having fun, and singing "Jesus Loves Me." Anyway, I somehow ended up going to a church camp that summer, and I believe it was because of that lady. My memory of the church camp is also vague, but I do remember that we had fun; it was in the forest, and there was a small lake. I have a few other vague memories, but the one thing that I remember the most is when a man took me out toward the center of the lake in a small rowboat. He was a good man who talked to me about Jesus and then asked me if I would like to invite Jesus into my heart. I didn't understand the significance of what was going on, but I said yes, and then he had me repeat the words of a prayer that invited Jesus into my heart. My memory of this event was secured because the man gave me a Bible and had me write down on the inner front page that I was saved along with the date. I had that Bible for many years, but somewhere along the way, I lost it.

Shortly after coming home from church camp that summer, I turned eight years old, and life was good; I had God in my life, and my family was still whole. It didn't take long for things to change: the lady that was sharing the gospel with the children of the neighborhood moved away, and my mom and dad got divorced. My mom had to start working, so thank God my grandma was there to take care of us kids; she had taken care of four kids of her own, and now she was taking care of five more. My grandma was a very good woman; I regret that I didn't fully realize and appreciate the influence she had on my heart until long after she had passed away. Sometimes at night, I could hear her praying; it was just a whisper, so I never understood what she was saying, but I truly believe that our lives were blessed because of her prayers. Like my grandma, my mom was also a very good woman who didn't deserve to end up in a broken marriage. My mom and grandma did the best they could, and with God's help, their best was truly remarkable: they overcame the difficulties of poverty by doing so much with very little, and they also instilled a sense of goodness in our hearts. They were godly/gracious people who successfully raised the five of us kids into adulthood. I remember getting teased by some of the other kids because they thought we were on welfare, but in reality, it was the grace of God working through my mom and grandma that sustained us and blessed us with the makings of a good heart.

My mom and grandma were always there for us kids, but children still need a dad, ideally a godly dad, and now we had neither. My dad moved out when I was nine years old, and without getting into the tragic details of betrayal, outside influences, and innocence lost, I will just say that by the time I was a young teenager, I had foolishly allowed Satan and his evil influence in the world to control many of my thoughts. I chose to do things that I knew were wrong even though my conscience continued to convict me.

A personal, spiritual relationship with Jesus Christ involves much more than a naive young boy repeating some well-thought-out words, but I will always be thankful for the exposure that I had to Christianity that summer, especially at such a young age, because it left a lasting impression on my heart. I'm very thankful that God never gave up on me; His amazing grace continued to call to me even though I strayed far from His Word.

As long as I can remember, I have always told myself that I believed in our Lord and Savior Jesus Christ. "For God so loved the world, that he gave his only begotten Son, that whosoever believeth in him should not perish, but have everlasting life" (John 3:16). Unfortunately, my childhood exposure to Christianity was choked off by unfavorable circumstances and my susceptibility to evil influences. As I grew older, I drifted far from any Bible studies or Christian fellowship, and the result was that I didn't really believe.

Once I wholeheartedly started to study and meditate on God's Word, I found myself looking more and more at the definitions of the original Hebrew and Greek words; I believe God has protected these words and their meanings. It's my understanding that the Hebrew and Greek languages of the Holy Bible are considered dead; this means that there is no one left that grew up speaking these languages. I don't believe it's an accident that these languages have been strictly preserved and taught as a second language. Consider that even the best English translations of the Holy Bible may not reflect the original significance of each and every verse, and sometimes we need help discerning the truth. Thank God we still have the ability to refer back to the original definitions of the Hebrew and Greek words.

My theological ignorance was revealed to me in part when I considered the Greek word that was translated to *believe* in the New Testament; it helped me realize that believing in Jesus Christ and relying on Him for salvation is why we have biblical faith. The Greek word that was translated to *believe* in the New Testament is *pisteuō* (Strong's #G4100), and this word is defined in the Strong's dictionary as "from 4102; to have faith (in, upon, or with respect to, a person or thing), i.e. credit; by implication, to entrust (especially one's spiritual well-being to Christ):—believe(-r), commit (to trust), put in trust with." The definition of *believe* in the context of our Christian belief is to have faith *in* Jesus Christ. Notice that the Greek word *pisteuō* is derived from a word that has the Strong's #4102 assigned to it; when you look that up, you find the word *pistis*, which is the Greek word translated to *faith* in the New Testament. These two Greek words are closely related; the people who truly believe *in* Jesus Christ will also have faith *in* Jesus Christ. Being established *in* the truth and moral standard of God's living Word/Jesus Christ is the fruit/evidence of our Christian belief/faith: the faith(fulness) *of* Jesus Christ will always be reflected

11

in the life of a true believer. This is the reason why I said earlier that I didn't really believe; I was telling myself that I believed in Jesus Christ, but I wasn't living a Christian life. "He that saith, I know him, and keepeth not his commandments, is a liar, and the truth is not in him" (1 John 2:4).

I was living the life of a fool by ignoring the most important blessing available to me. Many people throughout history suffered and died so that we could actually own a copy of the Holy Bible, but many of us have either ignored this blessing or remain ignorant of it. In the United States, back when I grew up, most of the families had at least one copy of the Holy Bible in their homes, but only God knows how many people took advantage of that blessing.

When I finally realized how desperately I needed God in my life, I decided that I was going to read the Holy Bible. Like many other people, I halfheartedly read parts of the Bible throughout my life, but this time was going to be different; I made a commitment to myself that I was going to read the whole Bible and try to understand it. I knew deep down in my heart (thoughts and feelings) that the most important thing in this life was to have a personal, spiritual relationship with our Lord and Savior Jesus Christ.

As I was reading through the Holy Bible, I began to question my worldly understanding of grace and faith. In the following scripture, the Word of God declares that we are saved by grace through faith and makes it very clear that it is the gift of God: "For by grace are ye saved through faith; and that not of yourselves: *it is* the gift of God" (Ephesians 2:8). With that in mind, I realized that our path to salvation can be greatly enhanced if we understand exactly what that means, so I decided to do a couple of studies, one on God's grace and the other on biblical faith. The results from these two studies are detailed on the following pages.

Chapter 1

God's Grace

†

Defining God's Grace

This study details my effort to understand God's grace. Satan's evil influence in the world creates an atmosphere of ignorance in which many people believe that God's grace is simply unmerited or undeserved favor. After I sincerely started to study and meditate on God's Word, I became very uncomfortable with that definition. It didn't take me long to discover that it was flawed, inadequate, and derogatory. The world continues to lead us astray, but if we respond to the calling of God's amazing grace, He will lead us to grace and truth.

> Be not thou therefore ashamed of the testimony of our Lord, nor of me his prisoner: but be thou partaker of the afflictions of the gospel according to the power of God; Who hath saved us, and called *us* with an holy calling, not according to our works, but according to his own purpose and grace, which was given us in Christ Jesus before the world began, But is now made manifest by the appearing of our Saviour Jesus Christ, who hath abolished death, and hath brought life and immortality to light through the gospel.
>
> 2 Timothy 1:8–10

Please read this study carefully, and you will see how it helped me understand the true meaning and significance of God's grace.

In my effort to understand God's grace, I considered the definitions of the Hebrew and Greek words that were translated to *grace* in the KJV of the Holy Bible. The following is a record of these two words and their definitions:

The Hebrew word that was translated to *grace* thirty-eight times in the Old Testament is *chen* (Strong's #H2580), and this word is defined in the Strong's dictionary as "from 2603; graciousness, i.e. subjective (kindness, favor) or objective (beauty):—favour, grace(-ious), pleasant, precious, (well-)favoured."

The Greek word that was translated to *grace* 130 times in the New Testament is *charis* (G5485), and this word is defined as "from 5463; graciousness (as gratifying), of manner or act (abstract or concrete; literal, figurative or spiritual; especially the divine influence upon the heart, and its reflection in the life; including gratitude):—acceptable, benefit, favour, gift, grace(-ious), joy, liberality, pleasure, thank(-s, -worthy)."

The following are the theological definitions of grace that I found in other dictionaries:

- The freely given, unmerited favor and love of God.

- The influence or spirit of God operating in humans to regenerate or strengthen them.

- A virtue or excellence of divine origin.

- Unmerited divine assistance given to humans for their regeneration or sanctification.

- The undeserved favor of God in providing salvation for those deserving condemnation.

- That which affords joy, pleasure, delight, sweetness, charm, loveliness: grace of speech.

- Good will, loving-kindness, favor of the merciful kindness by which God, exerting His holy influence upon souls, turns them to Christ, keeps, strengthens, increases them in Christian faith, knowledge, affection, and kindles them to the exercise of Christian virtues.

- The unmerited favor of God.

As you will see in the following pages, I continued to study and pray for the guidance of the Holy Spirit, and, eventually, my studies revealed and defined God's grace for me. As time went by, the Word of God was becoming more exciting, and my understanding continued to grow; I could truly feel the grace of God working inside of me. I finally reached a point in my studies where I felt like I had a good understanding of God's grace and His sanctifying power in our lives. Ultimately, my studies revealed the following definition of *God's grace* as one of the most accurate and comprehensive: *God's perfect loving character; God's graciousness (as gratifying), of manner or act (abstract or concrete; literal, figurative or spiritual;*

especially the divine influence upon the heart, and its reflection in the life; including gratitude); God's love in action; expressions of godliness or divine gifts; godliness/graciousness; divine character; the mannerisms and actions of God's love.

God's grace is His perfect loving character: God's graciousness (as gratifying), of manner or act, is manifested as expressions of godliness or divine gifts, and without a doubt, this is His love in action. It's important for each person to realize that every good and perfect gift is an expression of God's amazing grace that is constantly calling to us; if we sincerely respond through faith, we can freely receive the grace of the Holy Spirit. Salvation cannot be earned, but the grace of the Holy Spirit will have a divine influence upon our hearts, and the perfect loving character of Jesus Christ will be reflected in our lives. "For by grace are ye saved through faith; and that not of yourselves: *it is* the gift of God: Not of works, lest any man should boast. For we are his workmanship, created in Christ Jesus unto good works, which God hath before ordained that we should walk in them" (Ephesians 2:8–10).

Godliness/Graciousness

In my effort to understand the true meaning of God's grace, I spent many hours studying and meditating on God's Word. I also watched many sermons, read many commentaries, and prayed many times asking God for the guidance of His Holy Spirit. I finally concluded that God's grace is His expressions of godliness or divine gifts, and this led me to the understanding that the expressions of godliness or divine gifts are the fruit of His perfect loving character. I also realized that God's perfect loving character could also be expressed as godliness/ graciousness or divine character, and these words are also helpful when referring to Christians growing in God's grace and truth.

During my studies, as I was trying to understand God's grace, I watched a sermon that made me feel uneasy about my conclusion, so I decided to take another look at the Hebrew word in the Old Testament and the Greek word in the New Testament that was translated to *grace*. I noticed that the first word listed in both definitions was *graciousness*, so I looked up the word *gracious*. Thank God, Merriam-Webster was one of the dictionaries that I was using; it was very comforting for me to see the following listed as part of the definition: "obsolete: GODLY." I'm thankful that the word *godly* was listed, but it bothered me that it was listed as obsolete. I also looked up the word *gracious* in other dictionaries and did not find the word *godly* listed at all; it made me think that Satan is at work here. I wondered if the word *godly* was removed from the definition of *gracious* in the other dictionaries because of Satan's evil influence in the world. I feel that God led me to this discovery because it helps to validate all the studying that I've been doing. I hope that Merriam-Webster will never remove that very important part of the definition that informs people that graciousness is synonymous with godliness. I know I looked at these definitions more than once before, but at the time, I didn't realize that my studies on God's grace would also lead to godliness.

We can be sure that Satan's evil influence in the world is also involved in the process of scrutinizing and revising word definitions. The definition of *gracious* is a good example: the fact that God is gracious also confirms that gracious is godly, so obviously, the word *godly* should be the top defining word for *gracious*, but unfortunately, I was only able to find one modern-day definition of *gracious* that used the word *godly* as a defining word and it was classified as obsolete. Satan doesn't want the word *godly* used as a defining word for *gracious* because it's a revelation that God is gracious. The definition of marriage is another good example: God ordained marriage to be a holy union between one man and one woman, but unfortunately, every modern-day definition of marriage that I looked at was corrupted; for example, oxymoron language was added to include homosexual couples. Satan doesn't want the true meaning of marriage to be understood because holy marriages are the building blocks of a godly/gracious society. We need to be vigilant because the servants of darkness are striving to suppress and corrupt God's truth whenever they can. As Christians, we are the light of the world (Matthew 5:14); we should be striving to reveal and honor God's truth whenever we can. Satan's evil influence in the world also teaches us not to talk about the life-changing topics of politics or religion. How convenient for him that many people accept this, but the following is one of many examples of what the Word of God says: "And

20

he said unto them, Go ye into all the world, and preach the gospel to every creature" (Mark 16:15).

God's Graciousness (As Gratifying), of Manner or Act

It's very important that whatever I write concerning God's Word is true, so in an effort to make sure that my conclusion was accurate, I continued to study and pray for the guidance of the Holy Spirit. I finally realized that the best definition of God's grace that I could find comes from the Greek word *charis*. This, of course, makes perfect sense considering the fact that the Greek word *charis* was translated to *grace* in the New Testament. During my studies, I revisited this definition several times before I realized that it was using different words to basically describe the same understanding of God's grace that I received during my earlier studies. As I said earlier, I finally concluded that God's grace is His expressions of godliness or divine gifts, and this led me to the understanding that the expressions of godliness or divine gifts are the fruit of His perfect loving character. With that in mind, I was once again reading the definition of the Greek word *charis*, and I realized that when you analyze this definition, it actually declares God's perfect loving character in a very beautiful way. It also points out the different ways we can receive His expressions of godliness or divine gifts, especially the divine influence upon the heart and its reflection in the life, including gratitude.

The Holy Spirit also led me to the understanding that God's grace is His love in action, so basically the definition of the Greek word *charis* is declaring God's love in action. God's grace is the mannerisms and actions of His love, and God reveals Himself to us in and through His living Word/ Jesus Christ, so the grace of Jesus Christ is the mannerisms and actions of God's love. Please keep this in mind as you read through the following analysis of this very important and revealing definition:

The first thing we see when reading through the definition of the Greek word *charis* is "graciousness (as gratifying), of manner or act." The more we understand the extensive meaning of gracious, the more we'll be able to see how beautifully this phrase declares God's perfect loving character or God's love in action. In an effort to demonstrate this, I compiled the following list of words that are used in dictionaries to define *gracious* and added some brief definitions:

- GODLY: listed as obsolete in the Merriam-Webster dictionary.

- Kind: affectionate, loving; of a sympathetic or helpful nature; of a forbearing nature: gentle; arising from or characterized by sympathy or forbearance; of a kind to give pleasure or relief.

- Graceful: characterized by elegance or beauty of form, manner, movement, or speech.

- Benevolence: disposition to do good; an act of kindness; a generous gift.

22

- Courteous: marked by polished manners; marked by respect for and consideration of others.

- Indulging: to give free rein to; to take unrestrained pleasure in: gratify; to yield to the desire of; to treat with excessive leniency, generosity, or consideration.

- Beneficent: doing good or causing good to be done; conferring benefits; especially: performing acts of kindness and charity.

- Mercy: compassion or forbearance shown especially to an offender; a blessing that is an act of divine favor or compassion. Compassionate treatment of those in distress.

- Compassion: a feeling of deep sympathy and sorrow for another who is stricken by misfortune, accompanied by a strong desire to alleviate the suffering.

- Urbane: notably polite or polished in manner.

- Tact: a keen sense of what to do or say in order to maintain good relations and avoid offences.

The following includes three more brief definitions that can also help us with our understanding:

- Gratifying: giving pleasure or satisfaction: pleasing.

- Manner: a person's outward bearing; way of speaking to and treating others; a way of doing something; a characteristic or customary mode of acting: custom; a mode of procedure or way of acting: fashion; method of artistic execution or mode of presentation: style.

- Act: the doing of a thing: deed; something done voluntarily; a state of real existence rather than possibility; the process of doing: action; the sum of a person's actions or effects that serve to create an impression or set an example.

This is actually a very short and limited list. If you did a complete search of multiple sources and considered the synonyms, you could easily add many more wonderful words and definitions to this list, but surely you have a good idea of what a truly gracious person would be like. Now imagine all these words and their definitions in the perfect sense of godliness; you can clearly see how beautifully "graciousness (as gratifying), of manner or act" declares God's perfect loving character or God's love in action. When I realized that God's grace simply refers to His divine graciousness, it all made perfect sense: we are saved by grace through faith because God is gracious. The fact that God is gracious also confirms that godliness is synonymous with graciousness.

The next thing we see when reading through the definition of *charis* is "(abstract or concrete; literal, figurative or spiritual; especially the divine influence upon the heart, and its reflection in the life; including gratitude)." This part of the definition refers to the different ways we are able to receive God's grace: the expressions of godliness or divine gifts are manifested to us in a variety of ways. This includes all our physical and spiritual needs, especially the divine influence upon the heart and its reflection in the life, including gratitude. Through faith, the grace of God's Holy Spirit enables us to walk in newness of life. When Christians grow in grace (2 Peter 3:18), they're growing in the perfect loving character of Jesus Christ; His godly/gracious character will be reflected in their lives.

And the last thing we see when reading through the definition of *charis* is "—acceptable, benefit, favour, gift, grace(-ious), joy, liberality, pleasure, thank(-s, -worthy)." Besides the word *grace*, these other words were also translated from the Greek word *charis* on rare occasions when the context was referring to grace. In the KJV of the Holy Bible, the Greek word *charis* was translated to *grace* 130 times; it was only translated one time to *acceptable, benefit, gift, gracious, joy, liberality, thanked, and thankworthy;* it was translated two times to *pleasure*, three times to *thanks*, four times to *thank*, and six times to *favour*.

The definition of God's grace that was revealed to me earlier in my studies agreed with the definition of *charis*, so I decided to blend them: the definition of God's grace that was revealed to me as one of the most accurate and comprehensive is actually a blended definition. I believe it's helpful for people to understand that God's graciousness (as gratifying), of manner or act, is synonymous with God's perfect loving character, expressions of godliness or divine gifts, and God's love in action.

25

I also believe it's helpful for people to understand that God's grace is manifested as expressions of godliness or divine gifts in a variety of ways: (abstract or concrete; literal, figurative or spiritual; especially the divine influence upon the heart and its reflection in the life, including gratitude). God's perfect loving character can also be expressed as godliness/graciousness or divine character, and again, these words are also helpful when referring to Christians growing in God's grace and truth.

Unmerited or Undeserved Favor

Unfortunately, the most common definition I hear given for God's grace is unmerited or undeserved favor. As my understanding of God's grace grew, I realized that this definition was flawed and inadequate. The definition is flawed because the words *unmerited* or *undeserved* do not help us understand God's grace; these words only pertain to the human condition as it relates to receiving God's grace. "For all have sinned, and come short of the glory of God" (Romans 3:23). Consider this analogy: if you give someone a gold coin as a free gift, even though it is unmerited or undeserved because that person is filled with evil thoughts and has committed murder, rape, and many other crimes, does that mean that we now have to change the definition of the gold coin to the unmerited or undeserved gold coin? Of course not—that would be ridiculous; the gold coin is still defined as a gold coin whether that person deserved it or not. Also, the definition is inadequate because the word *favor* does not adequately define God's grace. Once

26

we remove the words *unmerited* or *undeserved*, all we are left with is the word *favor*. How can anybody believe that the single word *favor* adequately defines God's amazing grace? As we have clearly seen, God's grace is His perfect loving character: God's graciousness (as gratifying), of manner or act, is God's love in action, and this includes all of His expressions of godliness or divine gifts. When I realized that God's grace simply refers to His divine graciousness, it made me wonder how Satan's evil influence is able to keep so many people so confused and ignorant about something so obvious. Unmerited or undeserved favor does not define God's grace; however, it is definitely a benefit of God's grace that's available to each and every one of us.

The Manifestations of God's Grace

I'm very thankful for the following scripture because it describes God's amazing grace in a more comprehensive way: "As every man hath received the gift, *even so* minister the same one to another, as good stewards of the manifold grace of God" (1 Peter 4:10). The Greek word that was translated to *manifold* in this scripture is *poikilos* (Strong's #G4164), and this word is defined in the Strong's dictionary as "motley, i.e. various in character:—divers, manifold." I included this revealing scripture because it informs us that God's grace is various in character. God's grace includes everything He does or has done, in manner or act, so the various manifestations of God's amazing grace are omnipresent; for example, our lives

27

along with the miraculous bodies that we have all received are manifestations of God's amazing grace. "So God created man in his *own* image, in the image of God created he him; male and female created he them" (Genesis 1:27). It became clear to me that everything God created from the beginning are expressions of godliness or divine gifts supplying us with all our needs. "Every good gift and every perfect gift is from above, and cometh down from the Father of lights, with whom is no variableness, neither shadow of turning" (James 1:17). The sun that supplies us with light and warmth, the blue sky and the air that we all breathe, the moon and the stars that enhance the night sky, the clouds and rain, the mountains and valleys, the rivers and streams, the oceans and lakes, the forests and meadows, the multitudes of different animals, and the wide variety of delicious foods that we enjoy are all wonderful expressions of godliness or divine gifts. God's graciousness (as gratifying), of manner or act, is available to each and every one of us (Matthew 5:45), the manifestations of God's amazing grace are constantly calling to us. "But the God of all grace, who hath called us unto his eternal glory by Christ Jesus, after that ye have suffered a while, make you perfect, stablish, strengthen, settle *you*" (1 Peter 5:10).

Jesus Christ Is the Embodiment of God's Grace

My studies on God's grace clearly led me to the New Testament and the coming of our Lord and Savior Jesus Christ. The most important thing we need to know about God's grace is the fact that Jesus Christ is the embodiment of God's amazing grace: the grace of Jesus Christ is the mannerisms and actions of God's love. It's important to demonstrate the truthfulness of this statement and the accuracy of the blended definition of God's grace that was revealed to me during my studies, so I included the following examples:

"For the grace of God that bringeth salvation hath appeared to all men, Teaching us that, denying ungodliness and worldly lusts, we should live soberly, righteously, and godly, in this present world" (Titus 2:11–12). Notice how beautifully this scripture points to the first coming (Advent) of our Lord and Savior Jesus Christ and reveals that He is the grace of God that brings salvation. This makes perfect sense because Jesus Christ is God in the flesh, He is God's perfect loving character, He is God's graciousness (as gratifying), of manner or act, He is the ultimate expression of godliness, He is the ultimate divine gift, and He is God's love in action. We also read in this scripture that the grace of God (Jesus Christ) that brings salvation teaches us to deny ungodliness. Can we say or conclude then that ungodliness is the opposite or absence of grace? Would it be right to say "For the [perfect loving character or graciousness] of God that bringeth salvation hath appeared to all men."? We can clearly see that the definition fits the context of the scripture. "Jesus saith unto him, Have I been so long time with you, and yet hast thou not known me, Phillip? he that hath seen me hath seen the Father; and how sayest thou *then*, Shew us the Father?" (John 14:9).

29

"In the beginning was the Word, and the Word was with God, and the Word was God" (John 1:1). This amazing scripture testifies to the oneness of the Word/Jesus Christ and God. Again, our Lord and Savior Jesus Christ is God in the flesh, He is God's perfect loving character, He is God's graciousness (as gratifying), of manner or act, He is the ultimate expression of godliness, He is the ultimate divine gift, and He is God's love in action. Again, Jesus Christ is the embodiment of God's amazing grace.

> Hath in these last days spoken unto us by *his* Son, whom he hath appointed heir of all things, by whom also he made the worlds; Who being the brightness of *his* glory, and the express image of his person, and upholding all things by the word of his power, when he had by himself purged our sins, sat down on the right hand of the Majesty on high.
>
> Hebrews 1:2–3

The following is another amazing scripture that testifies to the fact that the Word/Jesus Christ was made flesh and dwelt among us: "And the Word was made flesh, and dwelt among us, (and we beheld his glory, the glory as of the only begotten of the Father,) full of grace and truth" (John 1:14). We also read in this scripture that the Word is full of grace and truth. How could we say "full of [unmerited or undeserved favor] and truth"? We can clearly see that the words *unmerited* or *undeserved* can never be applied to Jesus Christ. Also, how could we say "full of [favor] and truth"? That would be inadequate because Jesus Christ is God in the flesh. With that in mind, would it be right to say "full of [God's perfect loving character or God's graciousness] and truth"? Again, we can clearly see that the definition fits the context of the scripture.

"And the child grew, and waxed strong in spirit, filled with wisdom: and the grace of God was upon him" (Luke 2:40). Notice in this scripture that the grace of God was upon Him (Jesus Christ). How could we say "and the [unmerited or undeserved favor] of God was upon him"? Again, we can clearly see that the words *unmerited* or *undeserved* can never be applied to Jesus Christ. Also, how could we say "and the [favor] of God was upon him"? Again, that would be inadequate because Jesus Christ is God in the flesh. With that in mind, would it be right to say "and the [the perfect loving character or graciousness] of God was upon him"? And again, we can clearly see that the definition fits the context of the scripture.

"Of how much sorer punishment, suppose ye, shall he be thought worthy, who hath trodden under foot the Son of God, and hath counted the blood of the covenant, wherewith he was sanctified, an unholy thing, and hath done despite unto the Spirit of grace?" (Hebrews 10:29). Notice in this scripture that the Holy Spirit is identified as the Spirit of grace. This makes perfect sense because the Holy Spirit is the Spirit of God. How could we say "and hath done despite unto the Spirit of [unmerited or undeserved favor]"? We can clearly see that the words *unmerited* or *undeserved* can never be applied to the Holy

31

Spirit. Also, how could we say "and hath done despite unto the Spirit of [favor]"? That would be inadequate because the Holy Spirit is the Spirit of God. With that in mind, would it be right to say "and hath done despite unto the Spirit of [God's perfect loving character or God's graciousness]"? And again, we can clearly see that the definition fits the context of the scripture.

Notice in the following scripture that the people perverting God's grace are called ungodly men: "For there are certain men crept in unawares, who were before of old ordained to this condemnation, ungodly men, turning the grace of our God into lasciviousness, and denying the only Lord God, and our Lord Jesus Christ" (Jude 1:4). Again, can we say or conclude then that ungodly is the opposite or absence of grace? Would it be right to say "turning the [godliness/graciousness or divine character] of our God into lasciviousness"? And again, we can clearly see that the definition fits the context of the scripture. We can recognize true Christians by their fruit (Matthew 7:20), the godly/gracious character of Jesus Christ will be reflected in their lives.

"But grow in grace, and *in* the knowledge of our Lord and Saviour Jesus Christ. To him *be* glory both now and forever. Amen" (2 Peter 3:18). Notice that this scripture advises us to grow in grace. How could we say "But grow in [unmerited or undeserved favor], and *in* the knowledge of our Lord and Saviour Jesus Christ"? How do we grow in unmerited or un-deserved favor? We are either in favor or out of favor, we are either saved by our Lord Jesus Christ (grace through faith) or we're not. However, we can grow in the perfect loving character of Jesus Christ. Would it be right to say "But grow in [godliness/graciousness or divine character], and *in* the knowledge of our Lord and Savior Jesus Christ"? And again, we can clearly see that the definition fits the context of the scripture. To grow in grace is to grow in the godly/gracious character of our Lord and Savior Jesus Christ.

"Let no corrupt communication proceed out of your mouth, but that which is good to the use of edifying, that it may minister grace unto the hearers" (Ephesians 4:29). This scripture informs us that our speech can minister grace unto the hearers. How could we say "that it may minister [unmerited or undeserved favor] unto the hearers"? We can clearly see that this doesn't make any sense. Would it be right to say "that it may minister [godliness/graciousness or divine character] unto the hearers"? And again, we can clearly see that the definition fits the context of the scripture. When Christians share the gospel and speak in a righteous manner, God is working through them to build up the godly/gracious character of others.

All through the New Testament, you can find the word *grace* used many times like in the following scripture or used in a similar context: "The grace of our Lord Jesus Christ *be* with you all. Amen" (Romans 16:24). Would it be right to say "The [graciousness] of our Lord Jesus Christ *be* with you all. Amen"? The divine graciousness of our Lord and Savior Jesus Christ reflects God's perfect loving character or God's love in action, which is manifested as expressions of godliness or divine gifts, especially the divine influence upon the heart and its reflection in the life, including gratitude. And again, we can clearly see that the definition fits the context of the scripture.

So far, all the examples in this demonstration include scriptures quoted from the New Testament, but we can't ignore the Old Testament because we are all saved by God's grace through biblical faith. Our Lord and Savior Jesus Christ is the same yesterday, today, and forever (Hebrews 13:8), and the gracious character of the Lord never changes (Malachi 3:6), so I included a couple more examples with scriptures quoted from the Old Testament:

In the Old Testament, the word *grace*, for the most part, is used like it's being used in the following scripture or in a similar context: "But Noah found grace in the eyes of the Lord" (Genesis 6:8). Would it be right to say "But Noah found [godliness/graciousness or divine character] in the eyes of the Lord"? The Hebrew word that was translated to *found* in this scripture is *mâtsâ* (Strong's #H4672), and this word can also be defined as *to come forth to, to attain, find or acquire*, so we could also say "But Noah [attained or acquired] [godliness/graciousness or divine character] in the eyes of the Lord." Why else would God see grace in Noah? Noah believed the Word of God, and he relied on the Word of God for salvation, so he received a godly/gracious character which was the fruit/ evidence of his belief/faith(fulness). And again, we can clearly see that the definition fits the context of the scripture.

This is another example of how grace is used in the Old

Testament: "Surely he scorneth the scorners: but he giveth grace unto the lowly" (Proverbs 3:34). Would it be right to say "but he giveth [godliness/graciousness or divine character] to the lowly"? The Hebrew word that was translated to *lowly* in this scripture is *ānāv* (Strong's #H6035), and this word can also be defined as *humble, meek, and especially saintly*. The definition gives us some additional insight into the nature of these people. Apparently, the lowly are people who believe the Word of God and rely on the Word of God for salvation, so they have received a godly/gracious character which is the fruit/evidence of their belief/faith(fulness). Every good and perfect gift is from above (James 1:17), even our righteousness/faith(fulness). Again and again, we continue to see that the definition clearly fits the context of the scriptures.

These are all amazing scriptures with various degrees of significance, but for the purpose of this study on God's grace, I only focused on the fact that Jesus Christ is the embodiment of God's amazing grace and the accuracy of the blended definition of God's grace that was revealed to me during my studies. This is a very small sampling of the Holy Scriptures available for further study on this; please take the time to read the Holy Scriptures in a diligent and heartfelt manner, and you will clearly see the recurring evidence that our Lord and Savior Jesus Christ is the embodiment of God's amazing grace.

God's graciousness (as gratifying), of manner or act, is demonstrated and expressed in creation and throughout the Holy Scriptures by who God is and what He's done for us.

When we carefully consider all the information in this study, we can clearly see that God's grace is a revelation of His love: without a doubt, God's grace is the mannerisms and actions of His love, and God reveals Himself to us in and through His living Word/Jesus Christ, so the grace of Jesus Christ is the mannerisms and actions of God's love. "Thou therefore, my son, be strong in the grace that is in Christ Jesus" (2 Timothy 2:1).

That being said, let's take another look at the blended definition of *God's grace* that was revealed to me during my studies: *God's perfect loving character; God's graciousness (as gratifying), of manner or act (abstract or concrete; literal, figurative or spiritual; especially the divine influence upon the heart, and its reflection in the life; including gratitude); God's love in action; expressions of godliness or divine gifts; godliness/graciousness; divine character; the mannerisms and actions of God's love.* "But God, who is rich in mercy, for his great love wherewith he loved us, Even when we were dead in sins, hath quickened us together with Christ, (by grace ye are saved;) And hath raised *us* up together, and made *us* sit together in heavenly *places* in Christ Jesus" (Ephesians 2:4–6).

The grace (godliness/graciousness) of God and His living Word/Jesus Christ is reflected in our lives by the governing power and influence of the Holy Spirit, which is received through faith. "And of his fullness have all we received, and grace for grace" (John 1:16). As true Christians, we receive God's life-changing grace through faith, and then His divine grace is reflected in our lives: and *grace for grace*. But without faith, it's impossible to please God (Hebrews 11:6), so I hope you're looking forward to my second chapter on biblical faith. My studies on God's grace have helped me come to know the love of God in and through the graciousness of the Truth/Jesus Christ: to know the living Word of God/Jesus Christ is to know God/love. "Let us therefore come boldly unto the throne of grace, that we may obtain mercy, and find grace to help in time of need" (Hebrews 4:16).

Chapter 2
Biblical Faith
†

Defining Biblical Faith

This study details my effort to understand biblical faith. Satan's evil influence in the world creates an atmosphere of ignorance in which many people believe that Christian faith is blind. This insinuates that there's no evidence supporting the existence of God and that Christian faith is simply a blind belief that God exists. Nothing could be further from the truth, but unfortunately, many people are beguiled by whatever lies the world has to offer because they don't take the time to seek the knowledge of the Truth. "Be sober, be vigilant; because your adversary the devil, as a roaring lion, walketh about, seeking whom he may devour" (1 Peter 5:8). Please read this study carefully, and you will see how it helped me understand the true meaning and significance of biblical faith.

In my effort to understand biblical faith, I considered the definitions of all the Hebrew and Greek words that were translated to *faith or a derivative of faith* in the KJV of the Holy Bible. The following is a record of most of these words and their definitions:

The Hebrew word that was translated to *faith* one time and *faithful* three times in the Old Testament is *emuwn* (Strong's #H529), and this word is defined in the Strong's dictionary as "from 539; established, i.e. (figuratively) trusty; also (abstractly) trustworthiness:—faith(-ful), truth."

Another Hebrew word that was translated to *faith* one time, *faithful* three times, *faithfully* five times, and *faithfulness* eighteen times is *emuwnah* (H530), and this word is defined as "feminine of 529; literally firmness; figuratively security; morally fidelity:—faith(-ful, -ly, -ness, (man)), set office, stability, steady, truly, truth, verily."

Another Hebrew word that was translated to *faithful* one time and *faithfully* two times is *emeth* (H571), and this word is defined as "contracted from 539; stability; (figuratively) certainty, truth, trustworthiness:—assured(-ly), establishment, faithful, right, sure, true(-ly, -th), verity."

And another Hebrew word that was translated to *faithful* twenty times is *aman* (H539), and this word is defined as

a primitive root; properly, to build up or support; to foster as a parent or nurse; figuratively to render (or be) firm or faithful, to trust or believe, to be permanent or quiet; morally to be true or certain; once (Isa. 30:21; interchangeable with 541) to go to the right hand:— hence, assurance, believe, bring up, establish, + fail, be faithful (of long continuance, steadfast, sure, surely, trusty, verified), nurse, (-ing father), (put), trust, turn to the right.

40

We can clearly see that these Old Testament words are closely related by the spelling and the fact that the Hebrew words *emuwn*, the first word defined, and *emeth*, the third word defined, are derived from the Hebrew word *aman*, the fourth word defined, and the Hebrew word *emuwnah*, the second word defined is the feminine of the Hebrew word *emuwn*, the first word defined.

The Greek word that was translated to *faith* 239 times in the New Testament is *pistis* (Strong's #G4102), and this word is defined in the Strong's dictionary as

from 3982; persuasion, i.e. credence; moral conviction (of religious truth, or the truthfulness of God or a religious teacher), especially reliance upon Christ for salvation; abstractly, constancy in such profession; by extension, the system of religious (Gospel) truth itself: — assurance, belief, believe, faith, fidelity.

Another Greek word that was translated to *faithful* fifty-three times and *faithfully* one time is *pistos* (G4103), and this word is defined as "from 3982; objectively, trustworthy; subjectively, trustful: — believe(-ing, -r), faithful(-ly), sure, true."

We can clearly see that these two New Testament words are also closely related by the spelling and the fact that they're both derived from the same Greek word *peithō* (G3982), and this word is defined as

a primary verb; to convince (by argument, true or

41

false); by analogy, to pacify or conciliate (by other fair means); reflexively or passively, to assent (to evidence or authority), to rely (by inward certainty):—agree, assure, believe, have confidence, be (wax) conflent, make friend, obey, persuade, trust, yield.

As I considered all of these definitions, I realized that the usage of the word *faith*, like the word *grace*, increased significantly in the New Testament, so my studies on biblical faith, like God's grace, also led me to the New Testament and the coming of our Lord and Savior Jesus Christ.

The Greek word *pistis* that was translated to *faith* in the New Testament is by far the most dominating word used for *faith* in the Holy Scriptures. This New Testament word is also used when referring to the faith of the Old Testament heroes; Hebrews chapter 11 is a very good example of this and is often called "The Faith Hall of Fame." Based on my studies, the definition of the Greek word *pistis* is also the best definition of biblical faith that I could find. The following analysis of this very important and revealing definition will give us the insight needed to truly understand biblical faith:

The first thing we see when reading through the definition of the Greek word *pistis* is "persuasion, i.e. credence; moral conviction (of religious truth, or the truthfulness of God or a religious teacher)." It's very important that we have a clear understanding of what biblical faith is, so in an effort to help us understand the gist of what these words are actually saying, I included the following brief definitions:

42

- Persuasion: the condition of being persuaded; an opinion held with complete assurance; a deep conviction or *belief*; a system of religious *beliefs*.

- Credence: mental acceptance as true or real; *belief* as to the truth of something; something that establishes a claim to *belief* or confidence.

- Moral: of, pertaining to, or concerned with the principles or rules of right conduct or the distinction between right and wrong; expressing or conveying truths or counsel as to right conduct; conforming to a standard of right conduct or behavior.

- Conviction: a strong persuasion or *belief*; the state of being convinced; a fixed or firm *belief*.

After careful consideration, I believe the first part of this definition is saying that *faith is a firm belief in the truth and moral standard of God's living Word/Jesus Christ.* We believe because God's truth has persuaded and convinced us, we believe because we have mentally accepted God's truth as true or real, and we believe that God's truth is the moral standard. In this context, "(of religious truth, or the truthfulness of God or a religious teacher)" is referring to the truth of God's living Word. The living Word of God is truth, and God manifested His living Word of truth in the flesh as our Lord and Savior Jesus Christ: He is the Truth/Truth Itself. "Jesus saith unto him, I am the way, the truth, and the life: no man cometh unto the Father, but by me" (John 14:6). We firmly believe in Jesus

43

Christ as our Lord and Savior because He is the Truth and moral standard of God's living Word.

The next thing we see when reading through the definition of *pistis* is "especially reliance upon Christ for salvation; abstractly, constancy in such profession." Again, in an effort to help us understand the gist of what these words are actually saying, I included the following brief definitions:

- Abstract: expressing a quality or characteristic apart from any specific object or instance. Disassociated from any specific instance. Something that concentrates in itself the essential qualities of anything more extensive or more general.

- Constancy: the quality of being unchanging or unwavering, as in purpose, love, or loyalty; firmness of mind; faithfulness. Uniformity or regularity, as in qualities or conditions; invariableness. Steadfastness of mind under duress: fortitude.

Again, after careful consideration, I believe this part of the definition is saying that *faith emphasizes reliance upon Jesus Christ (the Truth) for salvation; steadfastly professed in the life by thoughts, actions, speech, and gratitude.* Our Christian belief/faith is a personal, spiritual relationship with Jesus Christ (the Truth), which emphasizes reliance upon Him for our salvation, and the fruit/evidence of this relationship is reflected in our lives by our thoughts, actions, speech, and gratitude. "For as the body without the spirit is dead, so faith without works is dead also" (James 2:26).

The next thing we see when reading through the definition of *pistis* is "by extension, the system of religious (Gospel) truth itself."

And again, after careful consideration, I believe this part of the definition is saying that *faith, by extension, is the system of religious (Gospel) truth itself: God's living Word/Jesus Christ, the moral standard of God's love.* We need to understand that our Lord and Savior Jesus Christ is the substance of the Gospel: He is the system of religious (Gospel) truth itself because *He is the Truth/Truth Itself,* so faith by extension is Jesus Christ. This makes more sense when we understand that the saving faith(fulness) of Jesus Christ is recorded in the Holy Bible as spiritual truth: the truth of Jesus Christ is perfect faith(fulness). This is a very important part of understanding biblical faith, so there will be more discussion on this as we move forward. "Beloved, follow not that which is evil, but that which is good. He that doeth good is of God: but he that doeth evil hath not seen God. Demetrius hath good report of all *men*, and of the truth itself: yea, and we *also* bear record; and ye know that our record is true" (3 John 1:11–12).

The last thing we see while reading through the definition of *pistis* is "—assurance, belief, believe, faith, fidelity." Besides the word *faith*, these other words were also translated from the Greek word *pistis* on rare occasions when the context was referring to faith. In the KJV of the Holy Bible, the

45

Greek word *pistis* was translated to *faith* 239 times; it was only translated one time to *assurance, belief, believe, believeth,* and *fidelity.*

Ultimately, my studies revealed the following definition of *biblical faith* as one of the most accurate and comprehensive: *A firm belief in the truth and moral standard of God's living Word/Jesus Christ, especially reliance upon Jesus Christ for salvation; steadfastly professed in the life by thoughts, actions, speech, and gratitude; by extension, the system of religious (Gospel) truth itself: God's living Word/Jesus Christ, the moral standard of God's love.* This definition basically says the same thing as the definition of the Greek word *pistis,* but this simplified version will help us spread the gospel because it's easier to articulate and easier for people to understand.

It's very important to understand exactly what this means. This understanding requires that we take a good look at biblical faith from two points of view, the saving faith *of* Jesus Christ/Truth Itself and the faith of Christians, which comes from being united with the saving faith *of* Jesus Christ/Truth Itself. "Even the righteousness of God *which is* by faith of Jesus Christ unto all and upon all them that believe" (Romans 3:22a).

The Saving Faith of Jesus Christ/Truth Itself

The definition of the Greek word *pistis* revealed that faith, by extension, is the system of religious (Gospel) truth itself, and this is referring to Jesus Christ because He is the substance

46

of the Gospel: He is the Truth/Truth Itself, so the saving faith(-fulness) of Jesus Christ is His truth, and if we turn that around, we can say that the truth of Jesus Christ is His saving faith(fulness). Jesus Christ, the only begotten Son of God, is the only one who was able to live a life in the flesh that was perfectly faithful to God the Father, and His faith(fulness) is recorded in the Holy Bible as spiritual truth, so the truth of Jesus Christ is perfect faith(fulness). This may seem confusing at first, but as we study and meditate on God's Word, the oneness of Jesus Christ, God's truth, and God's faith(fulness) become obvious. The following scriptures confirm that Jesus Christ is the embodiment of God's truth: He is the Truth/Truth Itself; this is a very important part of understanding biblical faith:

"Jesus saith unto him, I am the way, the truth, and the life: no man cometh unto the Father, but by me" (John 14:6). In this scripture, our Lord and Savior Jesus Christ (God in the flesh) declares that He is the Truth. All things were created by Jesus Christ (Colossians 1:16–17 and John 1:3); with that in mind, it makes perfect sense that the Creator of the universe is the Truth. The Creator is also the Way and the Life; He is the source of everything that is good and perfect, but for the purpose of this study on biblical faith, I'm currently trying to stay focused on the single fact that Jesus Christ is the embodiment of God's truth: He is the Truth/Truth Itself. "Thy word is true *from* the beginning: and every one of thy righteous judgments *endureth* for ever" (Psalm 119:160).

The following scripture informs us that the Word/Jesus

Christ is full of grace and truth: "And the Word was made flesh, and dwelt among us, (and we beheld his glory, the glory as of the only begotten of the Father,) full of grace and truth" (John 1:14). My studies on God's grace revealed that our Lord and Savior Jesus Christ is the embodiment of God's amazing grace. The fact that the Word/Jesus Christ is full of grace and truth confirms that He is also the embodiment of God's truth: again, He is the Truth/Truth Itself. "In whom ye also *trusted*, after that ye heard the word of truth, the gospel of your salvation: in whom also after that ye believed, ye were sealed with that holy Spirit of promise" (Ephesians 1:13).

"Study to shew thyself approved unto God, a workman that needeth not to be ashamed, rightly dividing the word of truth" (2 Timothy 2:15). This scripture identifies the Word of God/Jesus Christ as the word of truth. Our Lord and Savior Jesus Christ and the truth are one; they cannot be divided. "Of his own will begat he us with the word of truth, that we should be a kind of firstfruits of his creatures" (James 1:18).

"Sanctify them through thy truth: thy word is truth" (John 17:17). This scripture clearly identifies God's Word/Jesus Christ as His truth and makes it very clear that we are sanctified through His truth/Jesus Christ. Again, our Lord and Savior Jesus Christ and the truth are one; they cannot be divided.

"But when the Comforter is come, whom I will send unto you from the Father, *even* the Spirit of truth, which proceedeth from the Father, he shall testify of me" (John 15:26). In this scripture, our Lord and Savior Jesus Christ refers to the Holy

Spirit as the Comforter and the Spirit of truth. The Word of God/Jesus Christ (God in the flesh) is the Truth/Truth Itself, so the fact that He identifies His Holy Spirit (Galatians 4:6) as the Spirit of truth makes perfect sense. Don't overlook the fact that the Holy Spirit/Spirit of truth testifies of Jesus Christ/ Truth Itself. "Into thine hand I commit my spirit: thou hast redeemed me, O Lord God of truth" (Psalm 31:5).

"Then said Jesus to those Jews which believed on him, If ye continue in my word, *then* are ye my disciples indeed; And ye shall know the truth, and the truth shall make you free" (John 8:31–32). In this scripture, our Lord and Savior Jesus Christ makes it very clear that if we continue in His Word/ the Holy Bible/the Gospel, then we will come to know Him/ the Truth/Truth Itself, and being led by His Holy Spirit/Spirit of truth, we become free from the bondage and penalty of sin. "Lead me in thy truth, and teach me: for thou *art* the God of my salvation; on thee do I wait all the day" (Psalm 25:5).

These are all amazing scriptures with various degrees of significance, but for the purpose of this study on biblical faith, I only focused on the oneness of Jesus Christ and God's truth. This is a very small sampling of the Holy Scriptures available for further study on this; please take the time to read the Holy Scriptures in a diligent and heartfelt manner, and you will clearly see the recurring evidence that our Lord and Savior Jesus Christ is the embodiment of God's truth: He is the Truth/Truth Itself.

Again, and very noteworthy, the definition of the Greek

word *pistis* revealed that faith, by extension, is the system of religious (Gospel) truth itself. In this context, the word *extension* is clearly referring to "an enlargement in scope or operation," so if we're looking at the bigger picture, it should be understood that biblical faith is Truth Itself. If biblical faith is Truth Itself and Jesus Christ is the Truth, then biblical faith is Jesus Christ, and if we turn that around, we can say that Jesus Christ is biblical faith. Again, we need to understand that Jesus Christ, the only begotten Son of God, is the only one who was able to live a life in the flesh that was perfectly faithful to God the Father, and His faith(fulness) is recorded in the Holy Bible as spiritual truth, so the truth of Jesus Christ is perfect faith(fulness). "O Lord, thou *art* my God; I will exalt thee, I will praise thy name; for thou hast done wonderful *things; thy* counsels of old *are* faithfulness *and* truth" (Isaiah 25:1).

The definition of the Greek word *pistis* helped me understand that truth and faith are synonymous in Jesus Christ; He is also the embodiment of God's faith(fulness): He is the Truth and the Faith. This understanding was confirmed in my studies when I realized that sometimes the word *faith* is used in a context that refers to "*the system of religious (Gospel) truth itself: God's living Word/Jesus Christ, the moral standard of God's love.*" Especially when you see the word *faith* used with the definite article, "the faith" in the Holy Scriptures, this is the saving faith *of* Jesus Christ/Truth Itself, and other times it's used in a context that refers to "*A firm belief in the truth and moral standard of God's living Word/Jesus Christ, especially*

50

reliance upon Jesus Christ for salvation; steadfastly professed in the life by thoughts, actions, speech, and gratitude; by extension, the system of religious (Gospel) truth itself: God's living Word/Jesus Christ, the moral standard of God's love." This is the faith of Christians, which comes from being united with the saving faith *of* Jesus Christ/Truth Itself. The following scriptures confirm that Jesus Christ is also the embodiment of God's faith(fulness): He is the Truth and the Faith; this is another very important part of understanding biblical faith:

"But they had heard only, That he which persecuted us in times past now preacheth the faith which once he destroyed" (Galatians 1:23). Notice in this scripture that "the faith" is preached. In this context, it became clear to me that "the faith" is referring to God's Word/Jesus Christ/Truth Itself.

"But what saith it? The word is nigh thee, *even* in thy mouth, and in thy heart: that is, the word of faith, which we preach" (Romans 10:8). Notice in this scripture that "the word of faith" is preached. In this context, it became clear to me that "the word of faith" is referring to God's Word/Jesus Christ/ Truth Itself. As true Christians, "the word of faith" is near, even in our mouth (speech) and in our hearts (thoughts and feelings).

"O foolish Galatians, who hath bewitched you, that ye should not obey the truth, before whose eyes Jesus Christ hath been evidently set forth, crucified among you? This only would I learn of you, Received ye the Spirit by the works of the law, or by the hearing of faith?" (Galatians 3:1–2). Notice in these scriptures how it says "that ye should not obey the truth" and also how it says "or by the hearing of faith." In this context, it became clear to me that "the truth" and "the hearing of faith" are both referring to God's Word/Jesus Christ/Truth Itself.

"If thou put the brethren in remembrance of these things, thou shalt be a good minister of Jesus Christ, nourished up in the words of faith and of good doctrine, whereunto thou hast attained" (1 Timothy 4:6). Notice in this scripture that a good minister of our Lord and Savior Jesus Christ is "nourished up in the words of faith and of good doctrine." In this context, it became clear to me that "the words of faith and of good doctrine" are referring to God's Word/Jesus Christ/Truth Itself.

"Now to Abraham and his seed were the promises made. He saith not, And to seeds, as of many; but as of one, And to thy seed, which is Christ" (Galatians 3:16). "Wherefore then *serveth* the law? It was added because of transgressions, till the seed should come to whom the promise was made" (Galatians 3:19a). "But before faith came, we were kept under the law, shut up unto the faith which should afterwards be revealed" (Galatians 3:23). "Wherefore the law was our schoolmaster *to bring us* unto Christ, that we might be justified by faith" (Galatians 3:24). "But after that faith is come, we are no longer under a schoolmaster" (Galatians 3:25). Notice in verse 16 that to Abraham and *his seed* were the promises made, and that "his seed" is clarified as being singular and identified as being Christ: and to *thy seed*, which is *Christ*. Notice in verse 19 that the law was added because of transgressions until *the seed* should come to whom the promise was made. Now notice in verse 23 how it says that before *faith* came, we were kept under the law, shut up unto *the faith* which should afterwards be revealed. Notice in verse 24 that the law was our schoolmaster to bring us unto *Christ*, that we might be justified *by faith*. And finally, notice in verse 25 how it says after *that faith* is come, we are no longer under a schoolmaster. We can clearly see the synonymous relationship between "his seed," "thy seed," and "the seed" in verses 16 and 19, and "Christ" in verses 16 and 24, and "faith," "the faith," and "that faith" in verses 23, 24, and 25. In this context, it became clear to me that our Lord and Savior Jesus Christ is "the faith," which should afterward be revealed.

"For the love of money is the root of all evil: which while some coveted after, they have erred from the faith, and pierced themselves through with many sorrows" (1 Timothy 6:10). Notice in this scripture how it says "they have erred from the faith." In this context, it became clear to me that "the faith" is referring to God's Word/Jesus Christ/Truth Itself.

"By whom we have received grace and apostleship, for obedience to the faith among all nations, for his name" (Romans 1:5). Notice in this scripture how it says "for obedience to the faith." In this context, it became clear to me that "the faith" is referring to God's Word/Jesus Christ/Truth Itself.

"Examine yourselves, whether ye be in the faith; prove your own selves. Know ye not your own selves, how that Jesus Christ is in you, except ye be reprobates?" (2 Corinthians

13:5). Notice in this scripture how it says "whether ye be in the faith." In this context, it became clear to me that "the faith" is referring to God's Word/Jesus Christ/Truth Itself. This is also affirmed in the scripture when it says "Know ye not your own selves, how that Jesus Christ is in you." When the Word of God/Jesus Christ is in us, then we can be sure that we are in the Faith/Truth Itself.

These are all amazing scriptures with various degrees of significance, but for the purpose of this study on biblical faith, I only focused on the oneness of Jesus Christ, God's truth, and God's faith(fulness). This is a very small sampling of the Holy Scriptures available for further study on this; please take the time to read the Holy Scriptures in a diligent and heartfelt manner, and you will clearly see the recurring evidence that our Lord and Savior Jesus Christ is also the embodiment of God's faith(fulness): He is the Truth and the Faith.

The Word of God is the saving faith/spiritual truth of Jesus Christ; in other words, the spiritual truth of Jesus Christ is God's faith(fulness) to the world. The Holy Spirit also led me to the understanding that the faith(fulness) of God's truth is the moral standard of His love, and God reveals Himself to us in and through His living Word/Jesus Christ, so the truth of Jesus Christ is the moral standard of God's love that establishes our faith(fulness) and enables us to grow in grace.

The Faith of Christians

The faith of true Christians, which comes from being united with the saving faith *of* Jesus Christ/Truth Itself, is *"A firm belief in the truth and moral standard of God's living Word/Jesus Christ, especially reliance upon Jesus Christ for salvation; steadfastly professed in the life by thoughts, actions, speech, and gratitude; by extension, the system of religious (Gospel) truth itself: God's living Word/Jesus Christ, the moral standard of God's love."*

As Christians, our faith(fulness) comes from believing in Jesus Christ and relying upon Him for salvation. The Holy Bible is our physical representation of God's Word/Jesus Christ and His spiritual truth. Christians believe in Jesus Christ and rely upon Him for salvation by receiving Him as Lord and Savior, and this is done by receiving His spiritual truth, and when we receive His spiritual truth, we're receiving His Holy Spirit, which obviously includes, but is not limited to, His amazing grace and saving faith(fulness): believing is receiving.

The fruit/evidence of our faith(fulness) is steadfastly professed in our lives by our thoughts, actions, speech, and gratitude; the more spiritual truth we receive, the more gracious and faithful we become. By God's grace we are justified, sanctified, and glorified through the saving faith/spiritual truth of Jesus Christ: the Holy Spirit that comes with the saving faith/ spiritual truth of Jesus Christ unites us with God in love and purpose. The Holy Spirit leads us when we follow the spiritual truth of God's Word/Jesus Christ, and the Holy Spirit speaks to us when we listen to the spiritual truth of God's Word/Jesus Christ. Again, this is the faith of true Christians, which comes from being united with the saving faith *of* Jesus Christ/ Truth Itself. Being established *in* the truth and moral standard of God's living Word/Jesus Christ is the fruit/evidence of our Christian belief/faith: the faith(fulness) *of* Jesus Christ will always be reflected in the life of a true believer. "But he answered and said, It is written, Man shall not live by bread alone, but by every word that proceedeth out of the mouth of God" (Matthew 4:4).

Unfortunately, Satan's evil influence in the world creates an atmosphere of ignorance in which many people are deceived by worldly concepts and false doctrines. They ignore the calling of God's amazing grace by not seeking the knowledge of the Truth. "My people are destroyed for lack of knowledge: because thou hast rejected knowledge, I will also reject thee, that thou shalt be no priest to me: seeing thou hast forgotten the law of thy God, I will also forget thy children" (Hosea 4:6). Obviously, the knowledge of the Truth is very important. The context of the chapter where we find this scripture is dealing with lawlessness: a lack of righteousness/faith(fulness). This scripture also makes it very clear that the eternal consequences of sin can be passed on to our children if we don't raise them in the knowledge of the Truth. The lack of righteousness/faith(fulness) is the result of ignorance or the outright rejection of the truth and moral standard of God's living Word/Jesus Christ. Satan definitely has his loyal followers, but the overwhelming majority of lost people in the world are lost due to ignorance; for example, the people who don't believe in God and the people who believe in false gods are rejecting the only true God of the Bible by rejecting the truth and moral standard of His living Word/Jesus Christ. "There is a way which seemeth right unto a man, but the end thereof *are* the ways of death" (Proverbs 14:12).

Biblical Faith Is Not Blind

Fortunately, there are also many people who continue to believe and respond to the calling of God's amazing grace; they clearly see the grace of God's creation as absolute proof of His existence. "For the invisible things of him from the creation of the world are clearly seen, being understood by the things that are made, *even* his eternal power and Godhead; so that they are without excuse" (Romans 1:20). This scripture makes it very clear that biblical faith is not blind: the grace of God's creation declares the faith(fulness) of His spiritual truth. This scripture also makes it very clear that the people who choose not to see are without excuse. The available evidence guarantees that anyone seeking God in a diligent and heartfelt manner will be guided to the Christian faith, the system of religious (Gospel) truth itself: God's living Word/Jesus Christ, the moral standard of God's love.

The people who are truly responding to the calling of God's amazing grace will develop a strong desire for the spiritual truth of the Holy Scriptures. "Study to shew thyself approved unto God, a workman that needeth not to be ashamed, rightly dividing the word of truth" (2 Timothy 2:15). The people who study and meditate on the Holy Scriptures in a diligent and heartfelt manner will soon realize that the Holy Bible is in fact the true Word of God. Don't be deceived; our faith is not a blind leap into the darkness, it's a calculated step into the light. The Holy Bible has withstood the enduring test of time by proving itself to be completely faithful: the truth of God's living Word/Jesus Christ has been validated by a multitude of well-grounded facts. I'm very thankful that after so many years, I still had the opportunity to respond to the calling of God's amazing grace. The more you study and meditate on God's Word, the more you realize why the Holy Bible is by far the best-selling book of all time; this by itself is a good reason to believe that there's something very special about the Holy Bible. Unfortunately, some of the Bible translations have been corrupted by Satan's evil influence, so make sure you research the history of the English Bible; make sure you're using a tried and tested Bible translation.

"Remember the former things of old: for I *am* God, and *there is* none else; I *am* God, and *there is* none like me, Declaring the end from the beginning, and from ancient times *the things* that are not *yet* done, saying, My counsel shall stand, and I will do all my pleasure" (Isaiah 46:9–10). It's been reported by biblical scholars that the Holy Bible contains approximately 2,500 prophecies and that approximately 2,000 of them have been fulfilled, many with very specific details. "Now I tell you before it come, that, when it is come to pass, ye may believe that I am *he*" (John 13:19). The people who take the time to research the prophecies of the Holy Bible will discover an abundant amount of solid evidence that declares the divine authorship of the Holy Scriptures. "For the prophecy came not in old time by the will of man: but holy men of God spake *as they were* moved by the Holy Ghost" (2 Peter 1:21). Again, biblical faith is not blind: the spiritual truth of Jesus Christ is faithful. Without a doubt, we can firmly believe in the truth and moral standard of God's living Word/Jesus Christ, especially reliance upon Jesus Christ (the Truth) for salvation.

The people who do the research will also find that specific prophecies are noticeably absent from the other religious books that claim to be Scripture; this should be a major eye-opener to the honest skeptic.

> Let them bring *them* forth, and shew us what shall happen: let them shew the former things, what they *be*, that we may consider them, and know the latter end of them; or declare us things for to come. Shew the things that are to come hereafter, that we may know that ye *are* gods: yea, do good, or do evil, that we may be dismayed, and behold *it* together. Behold, ye *are* of nothing, and your work of nought: an abomination *is he that* chooseth you.
>
> Isaiah 41:22–24

The Holy Bible also contains many scientific facts and principles that were written thousands of years before the corresponding discoveries of secular science. For example, descriptions of the hydrological cycle were recorded in the Holy Scriptures thousands of years before it was fully understood and widely accepted by secular science. The following is just one of several scriptures that show stated knowledge of the hydrological cycle: "he that calleth for the waters of the sea, and poureth them out upon the face of the earth: The Lord *is* his name" (Amos 9:6b). The word *science* basically means knowledge, so this includes, but is not limited to, all the knowledge that God gave us concerning our physical and spiritual health. The people who take the time to research the scientific facts and principles that were recorded in the Holy Scriptures long before the corresponding discoveries of secular science will also discover an abundant amount of solid evidence that declares the divine authorship of the Holy Bible. And again, biblical faith is not blind: the spiritual truth of Jesus Christ is faithful. Without a doubt, we can firmly believe in the truth and moral standard of God's living Word/Jesus Christ, especially reliance upon Jesus Christ (the Truth) for salvation.

The reliability of the Holy Bible has also been confirmed by archaeological discoveries. For example, the 1947 discovery of the Dead Sea Scrolls is considered by some people to be the single most important archaeological manuscript find of all time; they prove that the Old Testament has been accurately persevered for over 2000 years. "Truth shall spring out of the earth; and righteousness shall look down from heaven" (Psalm 85:11). The people who take the time to research the relevant archaeological discoveries will also discover an abundant amount of solid evidence that declares the divine authorship of the Holy Scriptures. We continue to see that biblical faith is not blind: the spiritual truth of Jesus Christ is faithful. Without a doubt, we can firmly believe in the truth and moral standard of God's living Word/Jesus Christ, especially reliance upon Jesus Christ (the Truth) for salvation.

There are over 20,000 known manuscripts that document the New Testament text; this makes the New Testament the most reliable document of antiquity. The New Testament writings, before they were assembled, were circulated during the lifetimes of thousands of people who actually saw the miracles of Jesus and other historical events, but no one ever refuted the New Testament writings as fairy tales. Also, the following is considered to be special proof for the New Testament: the early Christians were strongly persecuted by both the Jews and the Roman government; if the writings of the New Testament were false, these two groups would have produced enough evidence to stop the growth of this sect, but none exists. "For the word of the Lord *is* right; and all his works *are done* in truth" (Psalm 33:4). The reliability of the Holy Bible is also supported by the documented proof of historians *and so much more*.

The Holy Bible used by most Protestants today is actually a remarkable collection of sixty-six books or letters (epistles) that were written by forty different writers over a period of roughly 1500 years. These writers were from all walks of life, from three different continents, and wrote in three different languages, yet the Holy Bible displays a consistent theme and unified message throughout the Holy Scriptures. "Every word of God *is* pure: he *is* a shield unto them that put their trust in him" (Proverbs 30:5).

There is also the evidence of the life-changing power of the Holy Spirit, which is received by God's grace through the saving faith/spiritual truth of Jesus Christ. There is more than enough evidence that declares the divine authorship of the Holy Bible. Again, the Holy Bible has withstood the enduring test of time by proving itself to be completely faithful: the truth of God's living Word/Jesus Christ has been validated by a multitude of well-grounded facts.

Pointing out all this evidence may seem unnecessary, but it's crucial for people to understand that biblical faith is not blind and that the Holy Bible is in fact the true Word of God. "The grass withereth, the flower fadeth: but the word of our God shall stand forever" (Isaiah 40:8). Many people are unaware of all this evidence because Satan's evil influence is working hard to keep them ignorant. By sharing this knowledge, the grace of God will work through us to call others to the saving faith/spiritual truth of His Word/Jesus Christ.

Biblical Faith Comes by Hearing the Word of God

Taking that crucial first step toward biblical faith and ultimately salvation may seem easy, but unfortunately, God is not a priority in the lives of many people. I hate to admit it, but I'm speaking from experience when I say that some people will not respond to the calling of God's amazing grace until they find themselves in a desperate situation, and only then, when they're urgently crying out for help will they seek God.

"Love not the world, neither the things *that are* in the world. If any man love the world, the love of the Father is not in him. For all that *is* in the world, the lust of the flesh, and the lust of the eyes, and the pride of life, is not of the Father, but is of the world" (1 John 2:15–16). These scriptures reveal why God is not a priority in the lives of many people. They either reject the truth and moral standard of God's living Word/Jesus Christ outright or they remain ignorant of the hopelessness of their situation because they have allowed themselves to be beguiled and preoccupied by the things that are in the world. Thank God people still have the opportunity to realize and acknowledge the hopelessness of their situation. They can still turn away from Satan's evil influence by sincerely seeking the righteousness of God. This decision seems to come easier for some and harder for others. The important thing is that we are still able to respond and that we do respond in a diligent and heartfelt manner. Unfortunately, there are many people who will never respond. "For God hath not called us unto uncleanness, but unto holiness" (1 Thessalonians 4:7).

The calling of God's amazing grace is our Lord and Savior Jesus Christ calling us to the saving faith(fulness) of His spiritual truth; He loves us and wants to have a personal, spiritual relationship with each and every one of us. Again, the Holy Bible is our physical representation of God's Word/Jesus Christ and His spiritual truth. Christians believe in Jesus

Christ and rely upon Him for salvation by receiving Him as Lord and Savior, and this is done by receiving His spiritual truth, and when we receive His spiritual truth, we're receiving His Holy Spirit, which obviously includes, but is not limited to, His amazing grace and saving faith(fulness): believing is receiving. When people truly respond to the calling of God's amazing grace, they will have a strong desire for the spiritual truth of the Holy Bible. Believing in Jesus Christ and relying upon Jesus Christ for salvation is directly proportional to believing in the spiritual truth of the Holy Bible and relying upon the spiritual truth of the Holy Bible for salvation.

The following scripture clearly states that faith comes by hearing and hearing by the Word of God: "So then faith *cometh* by hearing, and hearing by the word of God" (Romans 10:17). Jesus Christ is the living Word of God manifested in the flesh, so this scripture is making it very clear that faith comes by hearing what our Lord and Savior Jesus Christ is saying to us. The Holy Bible was written by holy men of God who wrote the Holy Scriptures by the inspiration of God. It's very important to understand that God/Jesus Christ is speaking directly to us throughout the Holy Scriptures. When we hear and believe/receive the Word of God, the saving faith/spiritual truth of Jesus Christ unites us with God in love and purpose. By God's grace, we receive our faith(fulness), which comes from the perfect faith(fulness) of Jesus Christ: He is the Faith, the saving faith that comes. "Create in me a clean heart, O God; and renew a right spirit within me" (Psalm 51:10). Our

Christian faith is our unity with the Word of God/Jesus Christ/ Truth Itself.

Satan's evil influence in the world has many people believing that the Old Testament is obsolete. "All scripture *is* given by inspiration of God, and *is* profitable for doctrine, for reproof, for correction, for instruction in righteousness: That the man of God may be perfect, thoroughly furnished unto all good works" (2 Timothy 3:16–17). These New Testament scriptures make it very clear that all scripture is given by inspiration of God. Obviously, the New Testament was still being written when the Apostle Paul wrote these scriptures, so he was clearly referring to the Old Testament scriptures as well. Also, the New Testament writers spent a considerable amount of time quoting or paraphrasing the Old Testament scriptures. Anyone who takes the time to sincerely study this will find it absolutely inconceivable how someone could conclude that the Old Testament is obsolete. Don't be deceived; again, it's very important to understand that God/Jesus Christ is speaking directly to us throughout the Holy Scriptures, and again, when we hear and believe/receive the Word of God, the saving faith/spiritual truth of Jesus Christ unites us with God in love and purpose. By God's grace, we receive our faith(fulness), which comes from the perfect faith(fulness) of Jesus Christ: He is the Faith, the saving faith that comes. "Wherefore lay apart all filthiness and superfluity of naughtiness, and receive with meekness the engrafted word, which is able to save your souls" (James 1:21). Our righteousness/faith(fulness) comes by believing/receiving God's living Word/Jesus Christ: God graciously gives us credit for the righteousness/faith(fulness) and born again status of Jesus Christ.

> For whosoever shall call upon the name of the Lord shall be saved. How then shall they call on him in whom they have not believed? and how shall they believe in him of whom they have not heard? and how shall they hear without a preacher? And how shall they preach, except they be sent? as it is written, How beautiful are the feet of them that preach the gospel of peace, and bring glad tidings of good things!
>
> Romans 10:13–15

The value of true preachers set apart by God cannot be overstated. It's very beneficial to hear sermons from a multitude of Spirit-led preachers. The Holy Spirit has blessed them with the ability to deliver God's Word with an enhanced degree of understanding. Spirit-led preachers will stay focused on Jesus Christ, and they will also display the Holy Scriptures on the screen whenever possible. Carefully consider the scriptures for yourself until you're satisfied that the preachers are trustworthy. "And Phillip ran thither to *him*, and heard him read the prophet Esaias, and said, Understandest thou what thou readest? And he said, How can I, except some man should guide me? And he desired Phillip that he would come up and sit with him" (Acts 8:30–31).

You will soon discover that there are many trustworthy preachers, and many of them will have dozens of sermons that you can watch or listen to. The saving faith *of* Jesus Christ comes by listening to Spirit-led preachers, studying the Word of God in a diligent and heartfelt manner, meditating on the Word of God, heartfelt prayer, and gratitude. The righteousness of our faith(fulness) is the fruit/evidence of a Spirit-led life. The worldly concepts and false doctrines will no longer be able to deceive us because God's living Word/Jesus Christ will lead us to the true knowledge of God.

> And the brethren immediately sent away Paul and Silas by night unto Berea: who coming *thither* went into the synagogue of the Jews. These were more noble than those in Thessalonica, in that they received the word with all readiness of mind, and searched the scriptures daily, whether those things were so.
>
> Acts 17:10–11

It's also very beneficial to listen to an audio Bible or listen and read along to an audio-video Bible. I like the King James Version of the Holy Bible narrated by the late Alexander Scourby, he did an excellent job, and I can tell you from experience, anyone who spends quality time with the Word of God on a regular basis will soon be able to recognize the saving faith/spiritual truth of Jesus Christ when they hear it.

Uniting with our Lord and Savior Jesus Christ is essential for our salvation, so we should be spending our time very wisely. "I am the vine, ye *are* the branches: He that abideth in me, and I in him, the same bringeth forth much fruit: for without me ye can do nothing" (John 15:5). We should be embracing God's living Word/Jesus Christ daily for spiritual strength and growth, but again, some of the Bible translations have been corrupted by Satan's evil influence, so make sure you research the history of the English Bible; make sure you're using a tried and tested Bible translation: if you haven't done so already, it's very important to watch some Spirit-led sermons on this topic.

> But the day of the Lord will come as a thief in the night; in the which the heavens shall pass away with a great noise, and the elements shall melt with fervent heat, the earth also and the works that are therein shall be burned up. *Seeing* then *that* all these things shall be dissolved, what manner *of persons* ought ye to be in *all* holy conversation and godliness.
>
> 2 Peter 3:10–11

The Saving Faith(fulness) of the Spirit/Truth

We live in a dimension of time and, like marriage, all love relationships that are mutually nurtured will grow stronger and stronger as time goes by. It's very important to understand that our righteousness/faith(fulness) comes from knowing and loving our Lord and Savior Jesus Christ. How can we believe in Jesus Christ and rely on Him for salvation if we don't know and love Him?

Spending quality time with the saving faith/spiritual truth of the Holy Bible is how we come to know and love Jesus

Christ. The saving faith/spiritual truth of Jesus Christ is our pathway to salvation. Notice in the following scripture that the Spirit is identified as truth: "Who is he that overcometh the world, but he that believeth that Jesus is the Son of God? This is he that came by water and blood, *even* Jesus Christ; not by water only, but by water and blood. And it is the Spirit that beareth witness, because the Spirit is truth" (1 John 5:5–6). It's very important that we have a basic understanding of the Holy Spirit so that we're not confused about our spiritual unity with God/Jesus Christ. This scripture and several others make it very clear that the Spirit is truth, so in other words, the Holy Spirit is the Spirit of truth. If the Spirit is truth and Jesus Christ is the Truth, then the saving faith/spiritual truth of Jesus Christ is an extension of God and His Holy Spirit. "And take the helmet of salvation, and the sword of the Spirit, which is the word of God" (Ephesians 6:17).

"It is the spirit that quickeneth; the flesh profiteth nothing: the words that I speak unto you, *they* are spirit, and *they* are life" (John 6:63). This is one of the most amazing scriptures: Jesus Christ (God in the flesh) declares that His words are spirit and they are life. Jesus Christ is the divine author of the Holy Scriptures, and His divinely inspired words are truth, so this scripture is also making it very clear that the Spirit is truth. Again, if the Spirit is truth and Jesus Christ is the Truth, then the saving faith/spiritual truth of Jesus Christ is an extension of God and His Holy Spirit. "For the word of God *is* quick, and powerful, and sharper than any two-edged sword, piercing even to the dividing asunder of soul and spirit, and of the joints and marrow, and *is* a discerner of the thoughts and intents of the heart" (Hebrews 4:12).

In the following scriptures, the Word of God continues to confirm that the Spirit is truth by referring to the Holy Spirit as the Spirit of truth:

> And I will pray the Father, and he shall give you another Comforter, that he may abide with you for ever; *Even* the Spirit of truth; whom the world cannot receive, because it seeth him not, neither knoweth him: but ye know him; for he dwelleth with you, and shall be in you. I will not leave you comfortless: I will come to you.
>
> John 14:16–18

"But when the Comforter is come, whom I will send unto you from the Father, *even* the Spirit of truth, which proceedeth from the Father, he shall testify of me: And ye also shall bear witness, because ye have been with me from the beginning" (John 15:26–27). "Howbeit when he, the Spirit of truth, is come, he will guide you into all truth: for he shall not speak of himself; but whatsoever he shall hear, *that* shall he speak: and he will shew you things to come. He shall glorify me: for he shall receive of mine, and shall shew *it* unto you" (John 16:13–14). Don't be deceived; when we believe/receive the saving faith/ spiritual truth of Jesus Christ, we're receiving the graciousness of the Holy Spirit/Spirit of truth (Spirit/truth).

The Holy Spirit/Spirit of truth (Spirit/truth) becomes our constant companion as we grow *in* the grace and truth of Jesus Christ: to grow *in* the grace and truth of Jesus Christ is to grow *in* the love of God's Holy Spirit. Unfortunately, there are far too many people preaching that the Holy Spirit is someone other than God the Father and His living Word/Jesus Christ/Truth Itself. Don't be deceived; as we have clearly seen, the Holy Spirit is the Spirit of truth, and Jesus Christ (God in the flesh) is the Truth/Truth Itself, so Jesus Christ is also the embodiment of God's Holy Spirit. "Now the Lord is that Spirit: and where the Spirit of the Lord *is*, there *is* liberty" (2 Corinthians 3:17).

The Holy Spirit is the essence of God's holy life, and the Spirit of truth is the life of the Truth/Jesus Christ that embodies the essence of God's holy life. The holy life (Spirit/truth) that's in and of God is the same holy life (Spirit/truth) that's in and of Jesus Christ. "But ye are not in the flesh, but in the Spirit, if so be that the Spirit of God dwell in you. Now if any man have not the Spirit of Christ, he is none of his" (Romans 8:9).

The Holy Spirit, the essence of God's holy life, is a spiritual fellowship that obviously includes, but is not limited to, God's breath of life and His mental disposition of grace and truth (love). When we believe/receive the living Word of God, the immortal and Holy Spirit of God, *in* and *through* the Truth/Jesus Christ, comes to us, dwells with us, comforts us, and sanctifies us.

The truth about the Holy Spirit can also be discerned by

71

taking a good look at the following scriptures:

> If ye love me, keep my commandments. And I will pray the Father, and he shall give you another Comforter, that he may abide with you for ever; *Even* the Spirit of truth; whom the world cannot receive, because it seeth him not, neither knoweth him: but ye know him; for he dwelleth with you, and shall be in you. I will not leave you comfortless: I will come to you. Yet a little while, and the world seeth me no more; but ye see me: because I live, ye shall live also. At that day ye shall know that I *am* in my Father, and ye in me, and I in you. He that hath my commandments, and keepeth them, he it is that loveth me: and he that loveth me shall be loved of my Father, and I will love him, and will manifest myself to him. Judas saith unto him, not Iscariot, Lord, how is it that thou wilt manifest thyself unto us, and not unto the world? Jesus answered and said unto him, If a man love me, he will keep my words: and my Father will love him, and we will come unto him, and make our abode with him.

John 14:15–23

The Greek word that was translated to *another* in the previous scriptures is *allos* (Strong's #G243), and this word is defined in the Strong's dictionary as "a primary word; 'else,' i.e. different (in many applications): — more, one (another), (an-, some an-)other(-s, -wise)." As we can clearly see, this Greek word doesn't necessarily mean *another*; in fact, the primary meaning is "'else' i.e. different (in many applications)," so in the context of the previous scriptures, I believe it should have been translated to *the Comforter in a different manner* instead of *another Comforter*. With that in mind, I believe Jesus is actually saying "And I will pray the Father, and he shall give you [the] Comforter [in a different manner], that he may abide with you forever." I believe this is also confirmed in the scriptures several times when Jesus says "I will not leave you comfortless: I will come to you." and when He says "and I will love him, and will manifest myself to him." and when He says "and we will come unto him, and make our abode with him."

Also, the Greek word that was translated to *comforter* in the previous scriptures is *paraklētos* (Strong's #G3875), and this word is defined in the Strong's dictionary as "an intercessor, consoler:—advocate, comforter." When we consider this brief definition in the context of our salvation, these five words can only apply to Jesus Christ. This Greek word was only used five times in the Holy Scriptures, and in the KJV of the Holy Bible, it was translated to the word *comforter* four times when referring to the Holy Spirit, but it was also translated to the word *advocate* one time when referring to Jesus Christ. Notice the context of how this Greek word is used in the following scripture: "My little children, these things write I unto you, that ye sin not. And if any man sin, we have an advocate with the Father, Jesus Christ the righteous" (1 John 2:1). There is not another comforter; Jesus Christ is the only Comforter. He was simply letting us know that He will come to us in a different manner: in the person of the Holy Spirit. "And because ye are sons, God has sent forth the Spirit of his Son into your hearts, crying, Abba, Father" (Galatians 4:6). Without a doubt, Jesus Christ is also the embodiment of God's Holy Spirit; He is the saving faith(fulness) of the Spirit/truth. "Jesus saith unto him, I am the way, the truth, and the life: no man cometh unto the Father, but by me" (John 14:6). The truth about the Holy Spirit is also declared by many other scriptures.

This is absolutely amazing; so far, my studies on God's grace and biblical faith have revealed our Lord and Savior Jesus Christ in the following ways:

- Jesus Christ is the embodiment of God's amazing grace: God's grace is the mannerisms and actions of His love, and God reveals Himself to us in and through His living Word/Jesus Christ, so the grace of Jesus Christ is the mannerisms and actions of God's love. The grace of Jesus Christ is God's perfect loving character, God's love in action.

- Jesus Christ is also the embodiment of God's truth and faith(fulness): biblical faith is Truth Itself, and Jesus Christ is the Truth/Truth Itself, so the truth of Jesus Christ is perfect faith(fulness). The Word of God is the saving faith/spiritual truth of Jesus Christ; in other words, the spiritual truth of Jesus Christ is God's faith(fulness) to the world.

- Jesus Christ is also the embodiment of God's Holy Spirit: the Spirit is truth, and again, Jesus Christ is the

Truth, so the saving faith/spiritual truth of Jesus Christ is an extension of God and His Holy Spirit. The Holy Spirit is the essence of God's holy life, and the Spirit of truth is the life of the Truth/Jesus Christ that embodies the essence of God's holy life. Jesus Christ, the Spirit/truth, is a spiritual fellowship that's in and of God, a spiritual fellowship that obviously includes, but is not limited to, God's breath of life and His mental disposition of grace and truth (love).

- The Holy Spirit also led me to the understanding that the faith(fulness) of God's truth is the moral standard of His love, and again, God reveals Himself to us in and through His living Word/Jesus Christ, so the truth of Jesus Christ is the moral standard of God's love that establishes our faith(fullness) and enables us to grow in grace.

As we can clearly see, the spiritual truth of the Holy Bible/God's Word is the actual faith (Spirit/truth) *of* Jesus Christ; this is why the Holy Bible is also referred to as the living Word and the Christian faith. The faith(fulness) of God's living Word/Jesus Christ is the system of religious (Gospel) truth itself: the spiritual truth of Jesus Christ is the Christian faith (biblical faith).

In the previous section, we took a good look at how biblical faith comes. It's very important to understand that the saving faith *of* Jesus Christ comes with the graciousness of His

Spirit/truth: when we receive the spiritual truth of Jesus Christ, we're receiving His Holy Spirit, which obviously includes, but is not limited to, His amazing grace and saving faith(fulness). Those of us who have truly received the saving faith (Spirit/truth) *of* Jesus Christ are the true believers; we continue to grow in His grace and truth because we continue to receive His mental disposition of grace and truth (love). This is how we come to know and love our Lord and Savior Jesus Christ; through His Spirit of truth, we abide *in* Him, and He abides *in* us. Everything we need for salvation is *in* and *of* the Truth/ Jesus Christ.

The True Significance of Biblical Faith

The following scripture continues to be misinterpreted by many people as the biblical definition for faith: "Now faith is the substance of things hoped for, the evidence of things not seen" (Hebrews 11:1). I also made that mistake, but during my studies, I realized that this scripture is a statement that simply declares that faith is the substance of things hoped for and the evidence of things not seen. The definition of biblical faith comes from understanding what *the substance is* and what *the evidence is,* and this understanding comes with the knowledge that God's Word/Jesus Christ/Truth Itself is the Faith.

The substance: As Christians, we should be able to declare the following with confidence: "Now [God's Word/Jesus Christ/Truth Itself] is the substance of things hoped for." The promises of God, which ultimately include the gift of eternal life, are what Christians hope for. There are thousands of promises in the Holy Scriptures, and Christians should have a clear understanding that these promises are received, or were received, by the grace of God our Father through the saving faith/spiritual truth of Jesus Christ because He is *the substance* of things hoped for.

The Greek word that was translated to *substance* in the previous scripture is *hupostasis* (Strong's #G5287), and this word is defined in the Strong's dictionary as "from a compound of 5259 and 2476; a setting under (support), i.e. (figuratively) concretely, essence, or abstractly, assurance (objectively or subjectively):—confidence, confident, person, substance." The definition shows us that this Greek word could also be translated to the word *person*. This is more evidence that the substance is a person and that person is Jesus Christ because He is the Faith. This Greek word was only used five times in the Holy Scriptures, and in the KJV of the Holy Bible, it was translated to the word *person* one time. Notice the context of how this Greek word is used in the following scripture: "Who being the brightness of *his* glory, and the express image of his person, and upholding all things by the word of his power, when he had by himself purged our sins, sat down on the right hand of the Majesty on high" (Hebrews 1:3).

The evidence: As Christians, we should also be able to declare the following with confidence: "Now [God's Word/Jesus Christ/Truth Itself] is […], the evidence of things not seen." As Christians, we should have a clear understanding that the saving faith/spiritual truth of Jesus Christ is also *the evidence* of things not seen. As we have seen earlier, the Holy Bible has withstood the enduring test of time by proving itself to be completely faithful: the truth of God's living Word/Jesus Christ has been validated by a multitude of well-grounded facts. The grace of God's creation also declares the faith(fulness) of His spiritual truth. The previous section titled "Biblical Faith is Not Blind" clearly points out an overwhelming amount of evidence that proves the spiritual truth of Jesus Christ is faithful. Without a doubt, the true significance of biblical faith is revealed in God's Word/Jesus Christ/Truth Itself because He is *the substance* of things hoped for, *the evidence* of things not seen, and so much more: He is the Creator of the universe and our God in the flesh.

"But without faith *it is* impossible to please *him*; for he that cometh to God must believe that he is, and *that* he is a rewarder of them that diligently seek him" (Hebrews 11:6). The people who diligently seek God will be guided to the Christian faith, and those who truly believe are rewarded with the faith (Spirit/truth) *of* Jesus Christ. The reason that it's impossible to please God without faith is because God's Word/Jesus Christ/Truth Itself is the Faith; in other words, we need to be spiritually united with our Lord and Savior Jesus Christ in order to please God. As true Christians, our Christian belief/faith is our unity with Jesus Christ. The reason that true Christians are able to please God is because they've been justified by the faith (Spirit/truth) *of* Jesus Christ. Again, we can clearly see that the true significance of biblical faith is revealed in God's Word/Jesus Christ/Truth Itself because He is the Faith, the saving faith that comes. The fact that true Christians are justified by the faith (Spirit/truth) *of* Jesus Christ is declared twice in the following scripture: "Knowing that a man is not justified by the works of the law, but by the faith of Jesus Christ, even we have believed in Jesus Christ, that we might be justified by the faith of Christ, and not by the works of the law: for by the works of the law shall no flesh be justified" (Galatians 2:16).

As Christians, it's very important that we understand the true significance of biblical faith in our own lives. True Christian belief *is* unity with the faith (Spirit/truth) *of* Jesus Christ: the reason that our Christian belief is also referred to as our Christian faith is because our Christian belief spiritually unites us with God/Jesus Christ in love and purpose, our Christian faith is the actual faith(fulness) *of* Jesus Christ, we abide *in* Him, and He abides *in* us. The faith (Spirit/truth) *of* Jesus Christ justifies us, sanctifies us, and glorifies us. I'm thankful for the following scriptures because they leave no doubt as to the source of our faith:

"Even the righteousness of God *which* is by faith of Jesus Christ unto all and upon all them that believe: for there is no difference: For all have sinned, and come short of the glory of God" (Romans 3:22–23).

"I am crucified with Christ: nevertheless I live; yet not I, but Christ liveth in me: and the life which I now live in the flesh I live by the faith of the Son of God, who loved me, and gave himself for me" (Galatians 2:20).

"But the scripture hath concluded all under sin, that the promise by faith of Jesus Christ might be given to them that believe" (Galatians 3:22).

"According to the eternal purpose which he purposed in Christ Jesus our Lord: In whom we have boldness and access with confidence by the faith of him" (Ephesians 3:11–12).

"And be found in him, not having mine own righteousness, which is of the law, but that which is through the faith of Christ, the righteousness which is of God by faith" (Philippians 3:9).

"And the grace of our Lord was exceeding abundant with faith and love which is in Christ Jesus" (1 Timothy 1:14).

"For they that have used the office of a deacon well purchase to themselves a good degree, and great boldness in the faith which is in Christ Jesus" (1 Timothy 3:13).

"Hold fast the form of sound words, which thou hast heard of me, in faith and love which is in Christ Jesus" (2 Timothy 1:13).

"And that from a child thou hast known the holy scriptures, which are able to make thee wise unto salvation through faith which is in Christ Jesus" (2 Timothy 3:15).

"That the communication of thy faith may become effectual by the acknowledging of every good thing which is in you in Christ Jesus" (Philemon 1:6).

"Here is the patience of the saints: here *are* they that keep the commandments of God, and the faith of Jesus Christ" (Revelation 14:12).

"Simon Peter, a servant and an apostle of Jesus Christ, to them that have obtained like precious faith with us through the righteousness of God and our Savior Jesus Christ" (2 Peter 1:1).

When we search the Holy Scriptures in a diligent and heartfelt manner, we continue to see that the true significance of biblical faith is revealed in God's Word/Jesus Christ/Truth Itself because He is the Faith.

"For I am not ashamed of the gospel of Christ: for it is the power of God unto salvation to every one that believeth; to the Jew first, and also to the Greek. For therein is the righteousness of God revealed from faith to faith: as it is written, The just shall live by faith" (Romans 1:16–17). These scriptures make it very clear that the righteousness *of* God that leads to salvation is revealed in the gospel of Christ from *faith to faith*. It's very important to understand that the gospel of Jesus Christ is declared throughout the entire Bible. God's Word/Jesus Christ/Truth Itself is God's faith(fulness) to the world, and our faith(fulness) is made perfect in the saving faith(fulness) *of* His Spirit/truth: from *faith to faith*. Every good and perfect gift is from above (James 1:17), even our righteousness/faith(-fulness).

Christian Belief/Faith

I love how the following scripture points out the fact that true Christians live *by* the faith *of* Jesus Christ: "I am crucified with Christ: nevertheless I live; yet not I, but Christ liveth in me: and the life which I now live in the flesh I live by the faith of the Son of God, who loved me, and gave himself for me" (Galatians 2:20). As Christians, we should have a clear understanding that the life that we now live, we live *by* the faith *of* Jesus Christ, and through diligent and heartfelt Bible study, we understand that this is referring to a Spirit/truth-filled life of faith(fulness). Living a Spirit/truth-filled life of faith(fulness) is synonymous with living *by* the Holy Spirit or *by* the faith (Spirit/truth) *of* Jesus Christ, and this starts with our Christian belief.

It's very important that we understand the unified relationship between our Christian belief and the faith (Spirit/truth) of Jesus Christ. Satan strives to keep the world in darkness, and unfortunately, he's been very successful. "Because strait *is* the gate, and narrow *is* the way, which leadeth unto life, and few there be that find it" (Matthew 7:14). Satan's evil influence in the world creates an atmosphere of ignorance, and this allows his evil deceptions to flourish. People are constantly being deceived because they're not receiving the knowledge of the Truth, and, consequently, their theology is being built upon worldly concepts and false doctrines. For example, many of the people throughout the world believe that Christian faith is blind; again, this insinuates that there's no evidence supporting the existence of God and that Christian faith is simply a blind belief that God exists. As we have clearly seen, this way of thinking is not biblical, it's totally false, and it's also very dangerous because it implies that Christian faith is something that comes from within one's own self instead of Jesus Christ. Unfortunately, there are also many well-meaning but misguided Christians who don't understand the Christian faith. Don't be deceived; we can't save ourselves. Christians need to understand what it means to have faith *in* Jesus Christ if they're going to understand the unified relationship between our Christian belief and the saving faith (Spirit/truth) of Jesus Christ.

Our Christian belief and the faith (Spirit/truth) of Jesus Christ are received together; it's impossible to receive one without the other. Spending quality time with the faith (Spirit/truth) of Jesus Christ causes us to receive our Christian belief/faith, that is, unless we reject the truth and moral standard of God's living Word outright like Satan and his fallen angels did. It's obvious that Satan and his fallen angels believe in God's existence, but they no longer believe in God's Word, so their belief is no longer mixed with faith(fulness). True Christians believe in God's existence, and they also believe in God's Word, so their belief comes mixed with the saving faith (Spirit/truth) *of* Jesus Christ. True belief in the gospel of Jesus Christ causes us to act accordingly.

Believing in Jesus Christ and relying upon Him for salvation is why we have biblical faith. Again, the Greek word that was translated to *believe* in the New Testament is *pisteuō* (Strong's #G4100), and this word is defined in the Strong's dictionary as "from 4102; to have faith (in, upon, or with respect to, a person or thing), i.e. credit; by implication, to entrust (especially one's spiritual well-being to Christ): — believe(-r), commit (to trust), put in trust with." The definition of *believe* in the context of our Christian belief is to have faith *in* Jesus Christ. Notice that the Greek word *pisteuō* is derived from a word that has the Strong's #4102 assigned to it; when you look that up, you find the word *pistis*, which is the Greek word translated to *faith* in the New Testament. These two Greek words are closely related; the people who truly believe *in* Jesus Christ will also have faith *in* Jesus Christ. Being established *in* the truth and moral standard of God's living Word/ Jesus Christ is the fruit/evidence of our Christian belief/faith: the faith(fulness) *of* Jesus Christ will always be reflected in the life of a true believer.

As true Christians, our Christian belief/faith is our unity with our Lord and Savior Jesus Christ: our Christian belief/ faith is literally *in* Jesus Christ. When Christians say "I have faith in Jesus Christ," they need to understand that their faith is *in* them because they are *in* Jesus Christ. This unified relationship is clearly seen in the following scripture: "That the communication of thy faith may become effectual by the acknowledging of every good thing which is in you in Christ Jesus" (Philemon 1:6).

Christian belief/faith can only be realized *in* Jesus Christ.

84

The following scripture makes it very clear that He is the author and finisher of our faith: "Looking unto Jesus the author and finisher of *our* faith; who for the joy that was set before him endured the cross, despising the shame, and is set down at the right hand of the throne of God" (Hebrews 12:2). Our Lord and Savior Jesus Christ is the only one who can establish and perfect our Christian belief/faith. The saving faith (Spirit/truth) *of* Jesus Christ is *in* Jesus Christ, so if we hope to receive His saving faith, we must become members of His body. Thank God that His Holy Spirit makes this possible; when our Christian belief/faith is established, the Holy Spirit unites us with Jesus Christ, and we become members of His body, we abide *in* Him, and He abides *in* us. "For as we have many members in one body, and all members have not the same office: So we, *being* many, are one body in Christ, and every one members one of another" (Romans 12:4–5).

All our blessings come from God/Jesus Christ, even our Christian belief. When we respond to the calling of God's amazing grace, we're responding to the faith (Spirit/truth) *of* Jesus Christ: the graciousness of the Truth/Jesus Christ is the love of God that causes us to receive our Christian belief along with His saving faith (Spirit/truth). Again, God graciously gives us credit for the righteousness/faith(fulness) and born-again status of Jesus Christ. This is our spiritual conception, the amazing moment of our justification, the amazing moment when we receive the earnest/seed of God's Holy Spirit, the amazing moment when God's living Word/Jesus Christ establishes our Christian belief/faith, and we become members of His true church: the fellowship of the Truth/Jesus Christ, the spiritual body of Jesus Christ. "Therefore if any man *be* in Christ, *he* is a new creature: old things are passed away; behold, all things are become new" (2 Corinthians 5:17).

At the moment when we're justified by our Lord and Savior Jesus Christ, He also begins to sanctify us. True Christian belief/faith is a sincere and lifelong commitment to receive and follow God's living Word/Jesus Christ/Truth Itself: the Holy Spirit becomes our constant companion as we grow in the grace and truth of Jesus Christ. Again, true Christian belief *is* unity with the faith (Spirit/truth) *of* Jesus Christ: the reason that our Christian belief is also referred to as our Christian faith is because our Christian belief spiritually unites us with God/Jesus Christ in love and purpose, our Christian faith is the actual faith(fulness) *of* Jesus Christ, we abide *in* Him, and He abides *in* us. The faith (Spirit/truth) *of* Jesus Christ justifies us, sanctifies us, and glorifies us. "Even the righteousness of God *which is* by faith of Jesus Christ unto all and upon all them that believe" (Romans 3:22a).

When we carefully consider all the information in this study, we can clearly see that God's truth, like God's grace, is also a revelation of His love: without a doubt, the faith(-fulness) of God's truth is the moral standard of His love, and God reveals Himself to us in and through His living Word/Jesus Christ, so the truth of Jesus Christ is the moral standard of God's love that establishes our faith(fulness) and enables us to grow in grace. "And with all deceivableness of unrighteous-ness in them that perish; because they received not the love of the truth, that they might be saved" (2 Thessalonians 2:10).

That being said, let's take another look at the definition of *biblical faith* that was revealed to me during my studies: *A firm belief in the truth and moral standard of God's living Word/Jesus Christ, especially reliance upon Jesus Christ for salvation; steadfastly professed in the life by thoughts, actions, speech, and gratitude; by extension, the system of religious (Gospel) truth itself: God's living Word/Jesus Christ, the moral standard of God's love.* "But the scripture hath concluded all under sin, that the promise by faith of Jesus Christ might be given to them that believe" (Galatians 3:22).

As true Christians, we are basically in a love relationship with God the Father and His living Word/Jesus Christ, so I hope you're looking forward to my third and final chapter on God's love. My studies on biblical faith have helped me come to know the love of God in and through the graciousness of the Truth/Jesus Christ: to know the living Word of God/Jesus Christ is to know God/love. "But thanks *be* to God, which giveth us the victory through our Lord Jesus Christ" (1 Corinthians 15:57).

Chapter 3

God's Love

†

Defining God's Love

As we have clearly seen, my studies on God's grace and biblical faith are both revelations of God's love, so my studies on God's love actually began with my studies on God's grace and then continued with my studies on biblical faith: the study of God's grace and biblical faith is the study of God's love. This chapter on God's love combines and continues my studies on God's grace and biblical faith by focusing on the unity of God's grace and truth, the graciousness of the Truth/Jesus Christ: the essence of God's love.

The Word of God declares that God *is* love (1 John 4:8 and 16). This truth is also revealed throughout the Holy Scriptures, so first and foremost, our Lord and Savior Jesus Christ is the embodiment of God's love, and the Holy Spirit is the Spirit of God's love. This means that all the true love in the world is in and of God and His living Word/Jesus Christ; this also means that true love is a moral love: the righteousness/faith(fulness) of God's grace and truth is a moral love. The gospel of Jesus Christ is the gospel of God/love. "And without controversy great is the mystery of godliness: God was manifest in the flesh, justified in the Spirit, seen of angels, preached unto the Gentiles, believed on in the world, received up into glory" (1 Timothy 3:16).

I am so thankful that the Holy Spirit guided my decision to choose God's grace and biblical faith as the topics of study for this book because God's love is revealed and defined by His grace and truth. Ultimately, my studies on God's grace and biblical faith revealed the following definition of *God's love* as one of the most accurate and comprehensive: *God is love; the fundamental principles of God's love are His grace and truth, and God reveals Himself/love to us in and through His living Word/Jesus Christ, so the grace of Jesus Christ is the mannerisms and actions of God's love, and the truth of Jesus Christ is the moral standard of God's love that establishes our faith(fulness) and enables us to grow in grace; the essence of God's love is the unity of His grace and truth, the graciousness of the Truth/Jesus Christ, the Spirit of the law.*

> Who shall separate us from the love of Christ? *shall* tribulation, or distress, or persecution, or famine, or nakedness, or peril, or sword? As it is written, For thy sake we are killed all the day long; we are accounted as sheep for the slaughter. Nay, in all these things we are more than conquerors through him that loved us. For I am persuaded, that neither death, nor life, nor angels, nor principalities, nor powers, nor things present, nor things to come, Nor height, nor depth, nor any other creature, shall be able to separate us from the love of God, which is in Christ Jesus our Lord.
>
> Romans 8:35–39

The Greek word that was translated to *love*, when referring to God's love, in the New Testament is *agape* (Strong's #G26), and this word is defined in the Strong's dictionary as "from 25; love, i.e. affection or benevolence; specially (plural) a love-feast: — (feast of) charity(-ably), dear, love." This definition defines God's love as "affection or benevolence." Notice that this type of affection is in the context of benevolence, and as we have seen earlier, benevolence is in the context of gracious: depending on the source, benevolence is sometimes used as either a synonym for gracious or as one of the words used to define gracious. Benevolence is about doing good for one another, so in this context, this type of affection is about caring for one another. Obviously, this definition clearly fits within the context of God's grace and truth (love). When we receive the faith (Spirit/truth) of Jesus Christ, the grace and truth of God's love will be reflected in our lives, and this definitely includes doing good for one another or caring for one another. Keep in mind, this also includes faithfulness because the truth of Jesus Christ is perfect faith(fulness).

Also, the definition then goes on to describe the "affection or benevolence" of God's love as "specially (plural) a love-feast." This is actually a very good and revealing description because the fellowship of the Holy Spirit is the ultimate love feast. Without a doubt, the grace and truth of Jesus Christ is God's love reaching out to embrace each and every one of us.

We are of God: he that knoweth God heareth us; he that is not of God heareth not us. Hereby know we the spirit of truth, and the spirit of error. Beloved, let us love one another: for love is of God; and every one that loveth is born of God, and knoweth God. He that loveth not

91

knoweth not God; for God is love.

1 John 4:6–8

The Word of God declares that we are saved by grace through faith, and as I said during my introduction, I realized that our path to salvation can be greatly enhanced if we understand exactly what that means. We now know that being saved by God's grace means that we're saved by the mannerisms and actions of God's love: the mannerisms and actions of Jesus Christ; and we now know that being saved through biblical faith means that we're saved through the moral standard of God's love: the saving faith/spiritual truth of Jesus Christ. God's moral love is the foundation of our personal, spiritual relationship with Jesus Christ, so we can be sure that it's also the foundation of all true love relationships.

Again, our Lord and Savior Jesus Christ is the embodiment of God's love, His grace and truth are the fundamental principles of God's love, and anything else that involves doing good for one another or caring for one another are the inner workings of God's love; it all fits together under the glorious umbrella of God's abundant love. As true Christians, we are abiding in the grace and truth of God's love: living by the faith (Spirit/truth) of Jesus Christ, so we should have, at the very least, a basic understanding of God's true love.

The Morality of God's True Love

God *is* love, so a firm belief in the truth and moral standard of God's living Word/Jesus Christ is a firm belief in God's love: true love will always be in perfect harmony with the truth and moral standard of God's living Word/Jesus Christ, so anti-Christ is anti-love. The system of religious (Gospel) truth itself, is the system of moral love that's in and of God/Jesus Christ.

The morality of God's true love can also be discerned by taking a brief look at the Ten Commandments. The first four commandments are about honoring our Heavenly Father; the fifth commandment is about honoring thy father and thy mother. As children, I believe the Spirit of the fifth commandment was also guiding us to honor the elderly, the people old enough to be our parents or grandparents, and ultimately our Heavenly Father. The Greek word that was translated to *honor* also means *to prize*, *to value*, and *to revere*. Notice that the other five commandments are mentioned in following scriptures:

> Owe no man any thing, but to love one another: for he that loveth another hath fulfilled the law. For this, Thou shalt not commit adultery, Thou shalt not kill, Thou shalt not steal, Thou shalt not bear false witness, Thou shalt not covet; and if *there be* any other commandment, it is briefly comprehended in this saying, namely, Thou shalt love thy neighbour as thyself. Love worketh no ill to his neighbour: therefore love *is* the fulfilling of the law.
>
> Romans 13:8–10

These scriptures make it very clear that *love is the fulfilling of the law,* so morality is naturally ingrained into the grace and truth of God's love.

The morality of God's true love fulfills the law. This is also confirmed by what our Lord and Savior Jesus Christ says in the following scriptures:

> Then one of them, *which was* a lawyer, asked *him a question*, temping him, and saying, Master, which *is* the great commandment in the law? Jesus said unto him, Thou shalt love the Lord thy God with all thy heart, and with all thy soul, and with all thy mind. This is the first and great commandment. And the second *is* like unto it, Thou shalt love thy neighbour as thyself. On these two commandments hang all the law and the prophets.
>
> Matthew 22:35–40

The Ten Commandments are the letter of the law, and the grace and truth of God's love are the Spirit of the law. The Ten Commandments, the letter of the law, is the schoolmaster, or the guide, that leads us to the Spirit of the law. "Wherefore the law was our schoolmaster *to bring us* unto Christ, that we might be justified by faith. But after that faith is come, we are no longer under a schoolmaster" (Galatians 3:24–25). As true Christians, we are now abiding in the grace and truth of God's love: living by the faith (Spirit/truth) of Jesus Christ, so we no longer need to be guided by the Ten Commandments because we are now guided by the Holy Spirit, the spiritual nature of God's love. "Who also hath made us able ministers of the new testament; not of the letter, but of the spirit: for the letter killeth, but the spirit giveth life" (2 Corinthians 3:6).

Unfortunately, Satan's evil influence has filled the world with counterfeit concepts of love, so it's very important that we understand the morality of God's true love. In an effort to demonstrate the difference between the morality of God's true love and Satan's counterfeit concepts of love, I included the following examples:

- God is love, so true love is a firm belief in the truth and moral standard of God's living Word/Jesus Christ; in contrast, a counterfeit concept of love is a claim of love that rejects the truth and moral standard of God's living Word/Jesus Christ.

- God is love, so true love is in perfect harmony with the truth and moral standard of God's living Word/Jesus Christ; in contrast, a counterfeit concept of love is a claim of love that disagrees with the truth and moral standard of God's living Word/Jesus Christ.

- God is love, so true love acknowledges the truth and moral standard of God's living Word/Jesus Christ; in contrast, a counterfeit concept of love is a claim of love that denies the truth and moral standard of God's living Word/Jesus Christ.

- God is love, so true love supports the truth and moral standard of God's living Word/Jesus Christ; in contrast, a counterfeit concept of love is a claim of love that hinders the truth and moral standard of God's living Word/Jesus Christ.

- God is love, so true love honors the truth and moral standard of God's living Word/Jesus Christ; in contrast, a counterfeit concept of love is a claim of love that disrespects the truth and moral standard of God's living Word/Jesus Christ.

- God is love, so true love embraces the sinners and graciously leads them to the truth and moral standard of God's living Word/Jesus Christ so that they can believe/receive the system of religious (Gospel) truth itself: God's living Word/Jesus Christ (Christianity), this way their worldly/carnal or sinful nature is overcome; in contrast, a counterfeit concept of love is a claim of love that embraces the sinners along with their worldly/carnal or sinful nature.

God *is* love, so it's impossible to think, do, or say anything in the name of true love that's contrary to the truth and moral standard of God's living Word/Jesus Christ. Unfortunately, and mistakenly, there are many people who claim to support evil behaviors in the name of love because the world has taught them that it's the loving thing to do, but this is a counterfeit concept of love because the spiritual nature of God's true love does not support evil behaviors: true love does not embrace the sinners along with their evil behaviors; true love embraces the sinners and graciously leads them to the truth and moral standard of God's living Word/Jesus Christ so that they can believe/receive the system of religious (Gospel) truth itself: God's living Word/Jesus Christ (Christianity), this way their evil behaviors are overcome. Supporting something in the name of love is the same as supporting it in the name of God, so it's impossible to support evil behaviors in the name of true love. Again, the righteousness/faith(fulness) of God's grace and truth is a moral love. "Woe unto them that call evil good, and good evil; that put darkness for light, and light for darkness; that put bitter for sweet, and sweet for bitter!" (Isaiah 5:20).

God's Holy Religion of Moral Love

True Christianity is God's holy religion of moral love; it's the only divine religion, so it's the only religion that can save us from our sins. As we have clearly seen, true Christianity is the only divine religion because it's the only religion that's in and of God and His living Word/Jesus Christ. "Jesus saith unto him, I am the way, the truth, and the life: no man cometh unto the Father, but by me" (John 14:6). Unfortunately, Satan's evil influence has also filled the world with false religions; this includes all the religions that claim to preach the divine truth, but instead are preaching something other than the divine truth, something other than the truth and moral standard of God's living Word/Jesus Christ. True Christianity separates us from the world; this obviously includes all the false religions. Unfortunately, and mistakenly, there are also many people who claim to support false religions in the name of love because the world has taught them that it's the loving thing to do, but this is another counterfeit concept of love because the spiritual nature of God's true love does not support false religions: true love does not embrace the sinners along with their false religions; true love embraces the sinners and graciously leads them to the truth and moral standard of God's living Word/ Jesus Christ so that they can believe/receive the system of religious (Gospel) truth itself: God's living Word/Jesus Christ (Christianity), this way their false religions are overcome.

Again, true Christianity is the only divine religion because it's the only religion that's in and of God and His living Word/ Jesus Christ, and God *is* love, so any other religion that claims divinity is a counterfeit concept of love *in and of itself*. True Christianity, God's holy religion of moral love, is derived from the system of religious (Gospel) truth itself: God's living Word/Jesus Christ, so true Christianity represents God's true church: the fellowship of the Truth/Jesus Christ, the spiritual body of Jesus Christ.

It's important to emphasize true Christianity, especially during a theological study, because Satan's priority is to destroy true Christianity, so along with all the other religions that are falsely claiming divinity, he has also established a counterfeit church: an evil parent organization that he falsely identified as Christian. "I considered the horns, and, behold, there came up among them another little horn, before whom there were three of the first horns plucked up by the roots: and, behold, in this horn *were* eyes like the eyes of man, and a mouth speaking great things" (Daniel 7:8). The little horn in this prophetic scripture represents Satan's counterfeit church. If you're unaware of the existence, or the identity, of Satan's counterfeit church, I strongly recommend that you take the time to watch some Spirit-led sermons on God's early church, Satan's counterfeit church, the Dark Ages, the Protestant Reformation, and the end times. Also, as I mentioned earlier, it's also very important to watch some Spirit-led sermons on the history of the English Bible, this research ties in with the Protestant Reformation. Spirit-led sermons on these topics are filled with Bible prophecies, especially those recorded in the books of Daniel and Revelation, and the documented proof of historians. God wants us to understand these topics, that's why He reveals them in His Holy Scriptures. Every Christian should understand these topics because it greatly enhances our Christian knowledge and maturity.

We have to be very careful and vigilant because Satan's evil influence is also attacking some of our local congregations from the top-down. In this fallen world, I strongly believe that local control structures over every aspect of our congregations will result in the least amount of corruption, especially if the congregations are set up as transparent fellowships in which all the members are treated as partners. Unfortunately, many of our local congregations are governed by the centralized control structures of the parent organizations, so in the worldly realm, they are controlled by either one person or a small group of people at the head of these parent organizations. Satan is well aware of this, so we can be sure that his evil influence has been working very hard to corrupt and control the one governing position or the small group of governing positions at the head of these parent organizations. This may be a new revelation for some of us, but Satan has been working on this for centuries, so we can be sure that he's been ruling over compromised parent organizations that are identified as Christian for a very long time, and we can also be sure that he's been slowly and deceptively implementing his worldly concepts and false doctrines into our local congregations from the top-down for a very long time.

Satan rules over his worldly kingdom in the same way, so we can be sure that his evil influence has also been working very hard to corrupt and control as many governing positions around the world as possible. This is how Satan rules over the international banking system (money), the mainstream media (information), the national governments (politicians: the visible ruling class), the international corporations (commerce), the pharmaceutical industry (drugs and vaccines), and almost all of the other major venues of power and influence. Satan utilizes centralized control structures because it's much easier to corrupt and control the people by corrupting and controlling the governing positions: the overwhelming majority of subordinates are usually submissive to the decisions handed down to them, especially if they need their jobs.

Satan's evil influence is also working very hard to create a one-world religious union. This worldly religious union is growing to include the religions that are falsely claiming divinity and the compromised parent organizations that are identified as Christian. This doesn't mean that all the people associated with these compromised parent organizations are lost: many of these people are being deceived because they are still babes in Christ; they simply haven't matured enough to know that many of the doctrines being taught by these organizations are anti-Christ. "As newborn babes, desire the sincere milk of the word, that ye may grow thereby" (1 Peter 2:2). Satan's evil influence has filled the world with confusion and deception, but if we continue to desire the sincere milk of God's Word, our personal, spiritual relationship with Jesus Christ will grow and develop into a mature relationship, a relationship that enables us to stand against the wiles of the devil (Ephesians 6:11).

Satan's one-world religious union is a worldly organization that's based on the religious tolerance of the worldly realm: the willingness to accept or allow beliefs, doctrines, and behaviors that are contrary to the truth and moral standard of God's living Word/Jesus Christ. The religious tolerance of the worldly realm is only tolerant of worldly religions, which includes counterfeit or compromised Christianity, but it does not tolerate true Christianity because true Christianity is in the spiritual realm: God's true church, the fellowship of the Truth/ Jesus Christ, is the spiritual body of Jesus Christ. Unfortunately, and mistakenly, there are also many people who claim to support this worldly religious tolerance in the name of love because the world has taught them that it's the loving thing to do, but again, this is another counterfeit concept of love because the spiritual nature of God's true love does not support this worldly religious tolerance. As we have clearly seen, God is love, so true love does not support anything that's contrary to the truth and moral standard of God's living Word/Jesus Christ.

Don't be deceived; Satan's counterfeit church, the evil parent organization that he falsely identified as Christian, is leading the effort to create his one-world religious union, and as we have clearly seen, this worldly religious union is also growing to include the compromised parent organizations that are identified as Christian. Keep in mind, Satan's priority is to destroy true Christianity, so in an effort to add to the confusion and the deception that's already surrounding Christianity, he also wants it to seem as if true Christianity is associated with his worldly religious union: Satan is counting on the ignorance of the world, he knows that the overwhelming majority of people in the world have no idea that he established a counterfeit church, they have no idea that this so-called church is an evil parent organization that he falsely identified as Christian, so a large percentage of these people will assume that this so-called church is legitimate. The same thing applies to the compromised parent organizations that are identified as Christian: the overwhelming majority of people in the world have no idea that these parent organizations are compromised, so a large percentage of these people will also assume that the compromised parent organizations that are identified as Christian are legitimate. Again, if you're unaware of the existence, or the identity, of Satan's counterfeit church, I strongly recommend that you take the time to do the research that I mentioned earlier.

Abiding in the grace and truth of God's love: living by the faith (Spirit/truth) of Jesus Christ, is the only way that we'll be able to navigate through all the confusion and deception that's in the world. As Christians, we should understand that it's impossible for true Christianity to be associated with Satan's one-world religious union because true Christianity is absolute and totally separate from the world: Satan's one-world religious union is in the worldly realm, and true Christianity is in the spiritual realm, in other words, they are incompatible. We should also understand that Satan's worldly system, which includes his one-world religious union, is only interested in persecuting true Christianity.

Again, true Christianity, God's holy religion of moral love, is derived from the system of religious (Gospel) truth itself: God's living Word/Jesus Christ, so true Christianity represents God's true church: the fellowship of the Truth/Jesus Christ, the spiritual body of Jesus Christ. "Enter ye in at the strait gate: for wide *is* the gate, and broad *is* the way, that leadeth to destruction, and many there be which go in thereat: Because strait *is* the gate, and narrow *is* the way, which leadeth unto life, and few there be that find it" (Matthew 7:13–14).

Being Born Again by God's Love

As Christians, most of us share a common belief that we're born-again as soon as we receive Jesus Christ as our Lord and Savior. As true Christians, this is true because God has graciously given us credit for the death, burial, and resurrection of Jesus Christ: we can claim born-again status *in* the body/fellowship of Jesus Christ because He was the firstborn from the dead, but personally, our spiritual birth process includes much more than many Christians realize. I heard the phrase "born-again Christian" many times throughout my life, and I knew what the common belief was, but I never really gave it much thought. After I finally started to study God's Word in a diligent and heartfelt manner, I slowly discovered, over a period of many years, that almost everything I learned in the secular world about theology was either wrong or deceptive.

With that in mind, I began to question the belief that we are personally born-again as soon as we receive Jesus Christ as our Lord and Savior. It didn't make sense to me because we have yet to shed our sinful flesh: we're still living in this fallen world, and our worldly/carnal bodies are still subject to death, so I was convinced that there had to be something more to it. I really wanted to understand this, but I didn't dwell on it because my previous experience with Bible study and revelation taught me to be patient, so instead, I continued to study and pray for understanding. Fortunately, I didn't have to wait very long; within a short period of time, God answered my prayers: one night, during a Bible study, I was wondering what Jesus meant when He was talking with Nicodemus about being born-again (John 3:1–10), and while doing so, I thought, maybe if I think about a natural birth it will help me understand what Jesus meant by a spiritual birth, and immediately I understood. Like most people, I knew that there are *three notable stages* involved in a person's natural birth process, and because of my theological studies, I also knew that there are *three notable stages* involved in a person's Christian salvation, so immediately my mind connected the relevant information, and I received the following revelation:

We are all born into this fallen world by a natural birth process that includes *three notable stages*: our natural conception, our natural development in the womb, and our natural birth; and likewise, as *true Christians,* we are all born-again into the kingdom of God by a spiritual birth process that also includes *three notable stages:* our spiritual conception, our spiritual development *in* the body/fellowship of Jesus Christ, and our spiritual birth. In biblical terms, these three notable stages are known as justification, sanctification, and glorification: our justification is our spiritual conception, our sanctification is a positional state of holiness *in* the body/fellowship of Jesus Christ in which we receive our spiritual development, and our glorification is our spiritual birth. To be saved by God's grace through biblical faith is to be personally born-again by the grace and truth of God's love.

Initially, when our Christian belief/faith is established, we are sealed with that Holy Spirit of promise; in other words, we are justified through the faith (Spirit/truth) of Jesus Christ: God graciously gives us credit for the righteousness/faith(fulness) and born-again status of Jesus Christ. This is the amazing moment when we receive Jesus Christ as our Lord and Savior, the amazing moment when our firm belief in the truth and moral standard of God's living Word/Jesus Christ is realized, especially our reliance upon Jesus Christ (the Truth) for salvation. The amazing moment of our justification is summarized by the following scriptures:

> In whom ye also *trusted*, after that ye heard the word of truth, the gospel of your salvation: in whom also after that ye believed, ye were sealed with that holy Spirit of promise, Which is the earnest of our inheritance until the redemption of the purchased possession, unto the praise of his glory.

Ephesians 1:13–14

I included the following definitions because they give us a better understanding of what happens at the amazing moment of our justification:

The Greek word that was translated to *sealed* in the previous scriptures is *sphragizō* (Strong's #G4972), and this word is defined in the Strong's dictionary as "from 4973; to stamp (with a signet or private mark) for security or preservation (literally or figuratively); by implication, to keep secret, to attest: —(set a, set to) seal up, stop." In the context of the previous scriptures, being "sealed" can also be defined as being *stamped with the private mark of God for security or preservation,* so the private mark of God is His stamp/seal of justification.

The Greek word that was translated to *earnest* in the previous scriptures is *arrhabōn* (G728), and this word is defined as "of Hebrew origin (6162); a pledge, i.e. part of the purchase-money or property given in advance as security for the rest:—earnest." The previous scriptures make it very clear that being sealed with that Holy Spirit of promise is the "earnest" of our inheritance. The phrase "that holy Spirit of promise" is future tense, so in this context, the word "earnest" is referring to *a part of the promise that is given in advance as security for the rest*, and the promise is clearly identified as the Holy Spirit, so the "earnest" of the Holy Spirit that is *given in advance as security for the rest* is the "seed" of God's living Word/Jesus Christ/Truth Itself. "Being born again, not of corruptible seed, but of incorruptible, by the Word of God, which liveth and abideth for ever" (1 Peter 1:23). During my studies, I realized that the "earnest" of God's Holy Spirit, *the Spirit of truth,* is synonymous with the "seed" of God's living Word, *the Word of truth.*

The private mark of God, His stamp/seal of justification, is the "seed" of His living Word/Jesus Christ/Truth Itself. Initially, when we receive Jesus Christ as our Lord and Savior, our Heavenly Father gives us the "earnest" of His Holy Spirit by planting the "seed" of His living Word in our hearts. Again, this is the amazing moment when our firm belief in the truth and moral standard of God's living Word/Jesus Christ is realized, especially our reliance upon Jesus Christ (the Truth) for salvation. "Now he that hath wrought us for the selfsame thing *is* God, who also hath given unto us the earnest of the Spirit" (2 Corinthians 5:5).

As we can clearly see, it's very important to understand the details surrounding our justification because they reveal when and how we receive the Holy Spirit. The following is another amazing scripture that declares the truth about our justification: "Now he which stablisheth us with you in Christ, and hath anointed us, *is* God; Who hath also sealed us, and given the earnest of the Spirit in our hearts" (2 Corinthians 1:21–22). *God has given/planted the earnest/seed of His Spirit/truth in our hearts.*

As Christians, we should strive to understand the full significance of our justification, and based on my studies, this includes an understanding of our justification in all three of the following ways:

- Our justification is our spiritual conception: when Jesus was talking with Nicodemus (John 3:1–10), He spoke about a new birth, a spiritual birth, and by doing so, He revealed the grand finale of what it means to be saved by God's grace through biblical faith. During their conversation, Jesus made it very clear that we "must be born again" in order to see, or enter into, the kingdom of God. Our spiritual birth is the fruit of a

108

divine process that can only be realized *in* the body/ fellowship of Jesus Christ; in other words, our personal born-again experience is the fruit of a *spiritual development* process *in* the body/fellowship of Jesus Christ that begins with our justification. Again, our justification is our spiritual conception.

- Our justification also establishes our sanctification *in* the body/fellowship of Jesus Christ: this is a positional state of holiness before God; we are now in the protective care of Jesus Christ. We are justified through the faith (Spirit/truth) of Jesus Christ: God graciously gives us credit for the righteousness/faith(fulness) and born-again status of the Jesus Christ.

- Our justification also establishes our personal, spiritual relationship with Jesus Christ: our relationship with Jesus Christ is personal because each person is unique, and each person has to personally respond to the calling of God's amazing grace. In other words, each and every person has to repent and believe/receive the system of religious (Gospel) truth itself: God's living Word/Jesus Christ. Our relationship with Jesus Christ is also spiritual because, *in* the body/fellowship of Jesus Christ, we are now part of a spiritual fellowship that's in and of God, a spiritual fellowship that obviously includes, but is not limited to, God's breath of life and His mental disposition of grace and truth, which is love.

The establishment of our personal, spiritual relationship with Jesus Christ also marks the beginning of our *spiritual development*: our sanctification *in* the body/fellowship of Jesus Christ is a positional state of holiness in which we are *also sanctified*. "Sanctify them through thy truth: thy word is truth" (John 17:17). We begin to live a life of repentance, a life that's contrary to the secular world around us; we begin to think differently, to think spiritually. As Christians, it should be obvious to all of us that we are currently in the sanctification stage of our spiritual birth process: we are in a positional state of holiness *in* the body/fellowship of Jesus Christ, and our spiritual development is ongoing.

Our spiritual birth process is a transitional process in which we are transitioning from our natural reality into a spiritual reality. It's a mystery, but we are currently in both realities at the same time. Our *spiritual development* is our growth *in* the body/fellowship of Jesus Christ; we're growing in His love because we're growing in His mental disposition of grace and truth. Our spirits, the essence of our *renewed minds*, are in the protective care of Jesus Christ, so *spiritually*, we're in a positional state of holiness, but at the same time, we have yet to shed our sinful flesh: we're still living in this fallen world, and our worldly/carnal bodies are still subject to death.

As true Christians, our connection with God is in and through His living Word/Jesus Christ; in other words, we are currently a part of God's spiritual fellowship because we're *in* the body/fellowship of Jesus Christ: we are totally reliant upon Jesus Christ for salvation. We can't see the Holy Spirit, but the fruit/evidence of the Holy Spirit will be reflected in our lives: we can't see the wind, but we can hear it, feel it, and see the effects of it. Being sealed with that Holy Spirit of promise was the earnest of our inheritance, so we have yet to receive the *sum* of our inheritance: our glorification, our personal born-again experience, is still in our future. Again, God has graciously given us credit for the death, burial, and resurrection of Jesus Christ: we can claim born-again status *in* the body/fellowship of Jesus Christ because He was the firstborn from the dead, but we are not personally born-again into the kingdom of God until Jesus Christ returns in bodily form and we receive our glorified/spiritual bodies.

The glorious return of our Lord and Savior Jesus Christ is described in the following scriptures:

> For the Lord himself shall descend from heaven with a shout, with the voice of the archangel, and with the trump of God: and the dead in Christ shall rise first: Then we which are alive *and* remain shall be caught up together with them in the clouds, to meet the Lord in the air: and so shall we ever be with the Lord. Wherefore comfort one another with these words.

> 1 Thessalonians 4:16–18

It will be during this glorious event when we will finally receive our glorification, our personal born-again experience. As Christians, we should understand that the dead *in Christ* are only dead in the worldly/carnal sense, but in reality, they are in a state of spiritual sleep; their spirits, the essence of their *renewed minds*, are in the protective care of Jesus Christ. When the dead *in Christ* are raised, the following will take place in the twinkling of an eye: their spirits, the essence of their *renewed minds*, will be awakened, and they will receive their new glorified/spiritual bodies as they are *personally* born-again into the kingdom of God; they will be caught up together in the clouds to meet the Lord in the air. Then, and also in the twinkling of an eye, the rest of us that are alive *in Christ* and remain, our spirits, the essence of our *renewed minds*, will receive our new glorified/spiritual bodies as we are *personally* born-again into the kingdom of God; we will also be caught up together with them in the clouds to meet the Lord in the air. The dead in Christ have already shed their sinful flesh, but for those of us who are alive *in Christ* and remain, it will be during this glorious event when we will finally shed our sinful flesh: we will no longer be living in this fallen world, and our bodies will no longer be subject to death. Again, Jesus made it very clear that we "must be born again" in order to see, or enter into, the kingdom of God: it will be during this glorious event when everyone *in Christ* will actually be able to see, and enter into, the kingdom of God.

Again, our spirits, the essence of our *renewed minds*, are currently in the protective care of Jesus Christ, so spiritually, we're in a positional state of holiness, but this was never meant to be our permanent position: in the context of our spiritual birth process, the church, the body/fellowship of Jesus Christ, acts like a womb, it's a temporary safe place in which our spiritual development is ongoing, but when the time is right, everyone in the church, the body/fellowship of Jesus Christ, will be *personally* born-again into the kingdom of God: the church will be lifted up to be with the Lord, and so shall we ever be with the Lord.

I believe we're all saved in this way by believing in the gospel of Jesus Christ. It's important to understand that the entire Bible is the gospel of Jesus Christ; it all guides us to our Lord and Savior. This is also confirmed by what Jesus said in the following scriptures: "Search the scriptures; for in them ye think ye have eternal life: and they are they which testify of me" (John 5:39). "For had ye believed Moses, ye would have believed me: for he wrote of me" (John 5:46). "And he said unto them, These *are* the words which I spake unto you, while I was yet with you, that all things must be fulfilled, which were written in the law of Moses, and *in* the prophets, and *in* the psalms, concerning me. Then opened he their understanding, that they might understand the scriptures" (Luke 24:44–45). The people who were saved before Christ was crucified were saved by believing in the Word of God, looking forward to the cross of Christ, and the people who were saved after Christ was crucified were saved by believing in the Word of God, looking back to the cross of Christ. The cross of Christ represents a moment in time for each and every believer; it represents the amazing moment of their justification: before our justification, we were living under the law, so we were being judged by the law, but after our justification, we are living under grace, so we are saved by God's grace through biblical faith. Again, to be saved by God's grace through biblical faith is to be personally born-again by the grace and truth of God's love.

That being said, let's take another look at the definition of *God's love* that was revealed to me during my studies: *God is love; the fundamental principles of God's love are His grace and truth, and God reveals Himself/love to us in and through His living Word/Jesus Christ, so the grace of Jesus Christ is the mannerisms and actions of God's love and the truth of Jesus Christ is the moral standard of God's love that establishes our faith(fulness) and enables us to grow in grace; the essence of God's love is the unity of His grace and truth, the graciousness of the Truth/Jesus Christ, the Spirit of the law.* "For God so loved the world, that he gave his only begotten Son, that whosoever believeth in him should not perish, but have everlasting life" (John 3:16).

As Christians, we are commissioned to preach the gospel of Jesus Christ, and as we have clearly seen, the gospel of Jesus Christ is the gospel of God/love, so in order to preach the gospel of Jesus Christ in a more effective manner we need to have, at the very least, a basic understanding of God's love and we need to be able to articulate that understanding. My studies on God's grace and biblical faith have helped me come to know the love of God in and through the graciousness of the Truth/Jesus Christ: to know the living Word of God/Je-

114

sus Christ is to know God/love. "Many will say to me in that day, Lord, Lord, have we not prophesied in thy name? and in thy name have cast out devils? and in thy name done many wonderful works? And then will I profess unto them, I never knew you: depart from me, ye that work iniquity" (Matthew 7:22–23). Unfortunately, and mistakenly, the overwhelming majority of people throughout history never found true love (God) because they spent their lives chasing after counterfeit concepts of love (Satan).

This book is a revelation of true love, a revelation of God's love, but it's also very important to understand the *love relationship* that we share with the Lord. Based on my experience, one of the best ways to grow in our love relationship with the Lord is to understand our love relationship with the Lord: the Holy Bible likens our personal, spiritual relationship with Jesus Christ to an ancient Jewish marriage, so if you haven't done so already, I strongly recommend that you take the time to watch some Spirit-led sermons on the ancient Jewish wedding traditions. "For this cause shall a man leave his father and mother, and shall be joined unto his wife, and they two shall be one flesh. This is a great mystery: but I speak concerning Christ and the church" (Ephesians 5:31–32).

Don't be deceived; true love will always be in perfect harmony with the truth and moral standard of God's living Word/ Jesus Christ, so anti-Christ is anti-love.

Bibliography

Merriam-Webster Dictionary, s.v. https://www.merriam-webster.com/.

Strong, James. *The new Strong's exhaustive concordance of the Bible: with main concordance, appendix to the main concordance, topical index to the Bible, dictionary of the Hebrew Bible, dictionary of the Greek Testament*. Nashville: T. Nelson Publishers, 1996.

9 781685 568290